The modern

GIRLHOOD AND GROWING UP

Lesley Johnson

OPEN UNIVERSITY PRESS
Buckingham · Philadelphia

To my sister, Pauline

Open University Press
Celtic Court
22 Ballmoor
Buckingham
MK18 1XW

and
1900 Frost Road, Suite 101
Bristol, PA19007, USA

First Published 1993

A catalogue record of this book is available from the British Library

ISBN 0 335 09998 X (pb)   0 335 09999 8 (hb)

Library of Congress Cataloging-in-Publication Data
Johnson, Lesley, 1949–
     The modern girl : social definitions of growing up in Australia in the 1950s and early 60s / Lesley Johnson.
          p. cm.
     Includes bibliographical references and index.
     ISBN 0-335-09999-8. — ISBN 0-335-09998-X (pbk.)
     1. Teenage girls—Australia.   2. Feminism—Australia.
3. Australia—Social conditions.   I. Title.
HQ799.A8J64   1993
305.42′0994—dc20   92–27016
                                                                   CIP

Typeset by Graphicraft Typesetters Ltd, Hong Kong
Printed in Great Britain by Biddles Limited, Guildford and King's Lynn

Contents

/ Preface

On the occasion of her turning 50, Germaine Greer wrote: 'All my life I've been trying to turn from being a girl into being a woman.' She claimed 'an unconquerable desire to grow up' and lamented that she felt 'as if I'm growing old without ever having grown up'.[1]* This book is about the obstacles to the fulfilment of this desire described by Germaine Greer – the desire to feel grown up as a woman.

The book focuses on social definitions of girlhood and growing up in the 1950s and early 1960s in Australia. During this period, normative definitions of what is involved in proper growing up began to acquire considerable force in organizing the lives of young women. The stories they told about what growing up entailed for the modern girl were both complex and frequently contradictory. My central preoccupation in looking at this material has been with the question, what does it mean for women to grow up? This is an issue that has interested me at a personal level ever since I left Sydney to take up my first major job at the age of 21. It's a question I have found myself contemplating at various moments since then as I have made changes to my life – or adapted to them – and moved cities several more times. This book does not provide an answer to this question; it is about why I, like Germaine Greer, find myself asking it.

It is a question, too, which, as I will show in the following chapters, is addressed at a number of levels in recent feminist debates about the project of feminism itself. It has arisen, in part, as a number of feminists have challenged the way a range of literature has represented women as developmental failures, as failing to undertake successfully the tasks of growing up. This work has had a

* Superscript numerals refer to numbered notes at the end of the book.

far-reaching impact within feminism itself, as it raises fundamental questions about the notions of the individual and personhood which have been central to some key texts of second-wave feminism. Feminist critiques of the dominance of masculine models of human growth and development seek to give voice to what is believed to be women's alternative experiences and modes of understanding the processes of growing up. Much of feminist theory in recent years has set out to build on this work and to define what it would mean for women as a group to grow up – to work towards an autonomous definition of womanhood in which these models of human development, and the notions of the individual and personhood that underlie them, play no part.

This book is an account of some of those historical factors and conditions through which Australian women have formulated the question, what does it mean to grow up? The book describes some of those shifting cultural patterns and norms through which modern Australian women have interpreted the meaning 'growing up' might have to them. It focuses on the 1950s and early 1960s as a period in which the processes of growing up for young people, and young women in particular, were being transformed in major ways. At another level, the book considers how the experiential problem of the meaning of growing up for modern women has conditioned and shaped the concerns of contemporary feminism. At least in part, second-wave feminism has been prodded into existence by the question of what adulthood means for women. The meaning this question has had for feminism has changed significantly over the past few decades. These shifts will be discussed in this book. It is my thesis, however, that it is time that the centrality of this question to the self-understanding of modern feminism be abandoned.

Acknowledgements

I would like to thank the following people for their assistance. Jennifer Laurence carried out much of the research for this project. Though I have not been able to infuse this book with her wonderful sense of humour, I have drawn on her insights and ideas about the project. Fiona Paisley, Julie Langsworth, Petrina Smith and Joanna Collard also gave me assistance in researching various parts of the book. Deborah Tyler and David McCallum provided useful comments on several chapter drafts, as well as generous friendship throughout the time of my working on this project. I am indebted to Dick Selleck for reading the early stages of this manuscript, as well as for his kindness and guidance over the years. John Docker read the final manuscript and made many valuable suggestions. I am very grateful to Patricia Bower for typing the final manuscript and, more generally, for her support in the final stages of my writing this book.

Research for the project was supported by a grant from the Australian Research Council and a Visiting Fellowship in the Research School of Social Sciences at the Australian National University enabled me to begin writing the book.

Finally, I want to express my gratitude to my family and friends for their warmth and encouragement. I am most deeply grateful to my sister, Pauline Johnson. She has given invaluable comments on several drafts of the manuscript and has been a wonderful intellectual and personal companion throughout the duration of my researching and writing this book.

Sources of illustrations

The author wishes to acknowledge permission to publish photographs from the following sources:

Introduction

> Why should a woman bother to be anything more than a wife and mother if all the forces of her culture tell her she doesn't have to, will be better off not to, grow up?
>
> Betty Friedan (*The Feminine Mystique*, 1983, p. 180)

In her book, described by so many as a 'revelation',[1] Betty Friedan declared there to be a crisis of women in the 1960s. It was, she argued, a 'crisis of women growing up'.[2] Material chains, she said, no longer bound women in post-Second World War America; all legal, political, economic and educational barriers to women's equality with men had been removed. The core of the problem facing women in the 1960s, she claimed, was 'a problem of identity'. Instead of women seeking to develop fully as individuals, to decide for themselves who they are and what they will be, the culture persuaded women, according to Friedan, that they should understand themselves not as 'persons', but as 'women'.[3]

Friedan identified American business interests as largely responsible for persuading women to understand themselves in this form. Manufacturers and advertisers, she argued, in their attempt to entice women into wanting more consumer goods for their homes in the years after the Second World War, developed 'the feminine mystique' as their weapon. These interests, Friedan claimed, set out to manipulate women's desires and needs and to seduce them into believing that through housework and the purchase of commodities they could express both their femininity and their individuality. 'The feminine mystique', she said, 'proclaimed full feminine achievement was to be found in being wife and mother.' In these roles, the American woman was to be respected as a full and equal partner to the American man in his world. But this mythology also pronounced American capitalism as a benevolent force enabling women to express themselves as individuals too: they could have everything they had ever dreamt of, it declared – they were free to choose cars, clothes, household appliances, and all the goods now on offer in the modern supermarket.

The explosive force of Friedan's book has been understood as lying in its capacity to give voice to 'the problem without a name'. She identified and sought to articulate for women this problem: the realization that such offers of material pleasures were not enough. The story she told, and hoped thereby to contribute to, was one of the beginning of an awakening of women. As a group, she claimed, they had been seduced in the 1950s into believing that their fulfilment lay in choosing to remain embedded in the traditional female roles of wife and mother: to remain simply 'woman'. The feminine mystique manipulated women's desires, confining their need for self-expression as individuals to the shallow and inauthentic choices offered to them by the marketplace. They did not seek to determine their own lives and identities. This, according to Friedan, was a refusal to grow up, a failure to become an individual in the modern world. An awakening of women would involve their accepting responsibility for themselves.

Friedan claimed to discern signs that women as a group were beginning to grow up. They were beginning to demonstrate that they wished to throw off the chains of the mistaken ideas imposed on them in the form of the feminine mystique. This dissatisfaction had first been noticed and articulated, Friedan suggested, at a popular level in the mass media in 1960, but had been trivialized and dismissed in that context. She sought, through the publication of her book, to give due weight and serious voice to this awakening, and in the process to enhance its potential to assist in the maturation of women.

The issues raised by Friedan's claims and the way in which they have been taken up in subsequent feminist debates form the organizing concerns of this book. Friedan's argument rested on a particular model of human growth and development and associated notions of identity formation, of the individual and adulthood. In seeking to explain why women failed, in her eyes, to achieve a fully adult identity, Friedan drew on and contributed to a developing critique of American capitalism and consumerism.[4] She claimed that women were persuaded to forfeit their identities and to accept the false promises of individuality proffered by the consumer society. She declared mass culture one of the evils of the modern world and lamented the particular susceptibility of women to its powers. And she juxtaposed the categories of 'woman' and 'person', identifying the former as a traditional identity and the latter as a modern one. According to Friedan, the awakening of women involved moving from the cosy but stunted existence of being defined by their embeddedness in the ascribed roles of wife and mother, to an embracing of the freedom and risks involved in becoming individuals in the modern world. The issues raised by these claims will be investigated throughout the course of the book, but my central preoccupation, and one which I see as summarizing all these concerns, is with the question I outlined in the Preface to this book of what it means for women to grow up.

Chapter 1 opens with a critical look at this story of the awakening of women – the story in Friedan's terms of the growing up of women as a group – as an account which continues to hold considerable force in popular and more academic understandings of the emergence and project of second-wave feminism.[5] In taking apart some of the key assumptions underlying this account, questions emerge about the relationship of women to the cultural ideal of the self-determining, autonomous individual considered to be central to what is often referred to as the project of modernity.[6] These major issues within recent feminist and social theory have shaped the preoccupations of this book. They will be explained in detail in Chapter 2 where I will also give an account of what is meant by the project of modernity in these debates.

Contemporary feminism suggests that women have a very particular relation to the cultural ideal of the self-determining, autonomous individual which, it has been claimed, confronts every modern individual with the task of making him or herself. Many feminists have radically questioned both the relevance of that project to women, as well as any possibility of maintaining its continuing legitimacy in contemporary social conditions. But, for the most part, feminist literature has failed to offer much by way of a sociological or historical elaboration of their claims. They have not explored the ways in which women's relationship to the notion of the self-determining, autonomous individual may change over time. To investigate these themes and to attempt to go some way towards redressing this historical lacuna in contemporary feminist debates, this book explores the terms in which the tasks of the modern individual – the tasks of making oneself – confronted, and were made accessible to, young Australian women in the 1950s and early 1960s. In this period, a wide range of institutions increasingly demonstrated a keen interest in defining how young women should make the transition from childhood to adulthood. These bodies all set out to define and transform what their growing up and girlhood involved in the modern world of post-war Australian society.

Contemporary understandings of the 1950s view that era as a time when women were forced out of the modern world, back into a traditional sphere of the duties of wife and mother. Such was the claim of Betty Friedan in her account of the 'crisis of women', and subsequent feminist histories of the emergence of second-wave feminism have tended to endorse this understanding of the period. The film 'Rosie the Riveter' gave popular force to this perception of the pre-history of second-wave feminism, but it also operates in an unproblematic way in a range of other texts.[7] I reassess this claim in asking what it means for women to grow up, both in terms of its characterization of the place of the 1950s in the history of the emergence and project of second-wave feminism and its constitution of the distinction between the 'traditional' and the 'modern' in the organization of women's lives.

It should be noted here that I am not attempting to provide a straightforward history of teenage girls in the 1950s and early 1960s. I am not claiming to discover what young women actually thought and did in this period. Nor is it my intention to write a history which will simply revive memories of that past in the way a number of popular texts have sought to do in recent years.[8] Though I hope many readers will find this book valuable for the context it provides for memories of their own growing up, its point is also to disturb or unsettle those memories. I am using historical evidence to make problematic contemporary understandings of the past and the present project of feminism. My approach has much in common with the notion of a history of the present as first outlined by Michel Foucault.[9] I do not seek out historical evidence to create a sense of the past, nor to make that past familiar. Rather, I am interested in gathering historical material as a means of exploring a different sense of our present than is currently dominant. My concern here is not to claim that I can provide a 'better' or 'truer' history than the genre of history which seeks to invoke popular memories of this era or than the previous feminist histories. I am proposing instead that the history I provide here may assist in constituting a different approach to the future of feminism and our understanding of the issues at stake when we ask what it means for women to grow up both as individuals and as a group.

In this book, I look at the spaces made available in the 1950s and early 1960s for young women to grow up in. These spaces were defined by a range of different institutions and their associated professionals, experts or spokespersons. This period is marked by an explosion of interest in re-forming and monitoring how young people should make this transition. Not all of these bodies spoke only of the lives and identities of young women. Some made statements about the responsibilities of the modern citizen, some about what growing up in the modern world entailed and some about the bountiful character of modern capitalism and the needs of national development. I am interested in how all such claims, and the practices built around them, converged to define what it meant for the modern young woman to grow up. Together, they did not necessarily constitute a coherent nor consistent account of what that process involved. Indeed, I am interested in the contradictions and tensions which existed between the different attempts to specify what that space should allow. I will seek to discuss the different stories told about the 'modern girl', the pleasures they offered or intimated – and hence, the force they contained for making sense to young women of what their growing up entailed in the modern world.

In looking at these different spaces – at the different vocabularies made available to young women to understand and evaluate their lives and themselves – I will often be looking at material which does not mention 'women' or 'girls' at all. In the following section, I address the issues such material poses for writing a feminist history, and, in particular, I explore its implications in relationship to contemporary feminist work in the history of education. Little has been written to date about the history of girlhood, but recent historical work on women's education has at least begun to open up this field. I want to point, however, to some problems in this work which need to be addressed in thinking about what is involved in writing a feminist history of girlhood and growing up.

A feminist history of girlhood and growing up

The distinctions between women's history and feminist history have been well rehearsed in recent years. In the Australian context, Jill Matthews has distinguished between these two projects on a number of levels. Women's history seeks to add women into traditional historical investigation; to make them visible. Matthews characterizes this approach as 'contribution history' and distinguishes it from feminist history which seeks to change the whole nature of historical investigation itself. Feminist history constitutes a fundamental challenge to the historical enterprise with its insistence on the centrality of gender relations as a major dynamic within history. 'Feminist history,' she adds, 'in fact, need not focus on women as such, although in general it has done so.'[10] She notes, too, that we must recognize that any history of 'woman' is a fantasy, that we need to study the diversity of women's experience.[11]

But these claims have their own dangers. Denise Riley has shown how not only the category 'woman' but the category of 'women' too is troublesome. She suggests that while feminism must necessarily speak of 'women', it must also maintain an active scepticism about the category itself. Feminism needs always to be challenging and refurbishing the category 'women', rather than strengthening it. Riley argues that the category 'women' has been an important one at the collective level at various points in history in forming a politics of identity through which women have sought to achieve political objectives. Speaking 'as women', they have sought to protest against and change the ways in which their lives are organized and determined by being designated 'women'. But there is nothing inherently radical or progressive, she points out, about appeals to the category 'women'. Public invocations of the difference of 'women' can be used for a whole range of political purposes. At times, then, feminists have distanced themselves from this category, refused to be defined as 'women'; at other times, they have sought to lay claim to this identity. This apparent inconsistency, Riley argues, is not a problem. On the contrary, it is inescapable; this instability should be embraced rather than ignored or denied. It is this capacity to deal with the designation 'women' with irony and reflexivity, she claims, which will distinguish feminist from conservative uses of the term.

Thus, although it is now generally agreed that feminist history should not seek simply to make women visible, to fish up heroines to put alongside the heroes (be they the great men or the authentic working-class ones), Riley's analysis suggests that we need to ask whether there is still not a tendency in feminist writings to speak of 'women' (and 'men') in such a way as to strengthen these categories rather than to challenge them. Studies of femininity and masculinity need to avoid presenting their historical forms as somehow arbitrary, if not distorting, moulds placed over the real women and men who continue on throughout history. Riley makes a similar point, referring to the sort of history which writes 'as if men and women are the same actors wearing different costumes from scene to scene but whose clashes are always the same'.[12]

Riley warns that feminist history should avoid assuming 'in advance', that which 'really we needed to catch, instead, on the wings of its formulation'.[13] Joan Wallach Scott similarly argues for the necessity of taking an approach which calls into question 'the reliability of terms that have been taken as self-evident by historicizing them'. The story which feminist historians should seek to tell, she suggests, is 'no longer about the things that have happened to women and men and how they have reacted to them; instead it is about how the subjective and collective meanings of women and men as categories of identity have been constructed'. Instead of seeing women as always already powerless victims, objects who defend themselves against men as subjects who oppress, feminist history needs to investigate the material and ideological specificities of any particular moment which constitute a group of women as powerless or subordinate.[14] These points can be explained more clearly in relation to the historiography of women's education.

To date, there are few feminist histories of the schooling of young women in Australia or elsewhere, but for the 1950s they are virtually non-existent. The pieces of work that do exist, though useful in terms of their attempt to begin to map out the field, nevertheless fail most notably to make problematic the category 'women'. On the contrary, they are very much the sort of histories criticized above, which assume that young women exist as a group outside history and look to find the distorting influences and the false ideas which existed about them, or were imposed on them, in the past.

Lucy Bland and others, for instance, in a pioneering paper published in 1979 about the ideology of femininity in 1950s England, write of 'both official and popular ideologies of girls' education throughout this period stress[ing] the primacy of women's domestic role'.[15] Similarly, Ann Marie Wolpe, analysing three key English education policy documents published between 1944 and 1963, points to their preoccupation with preparing young women for their futures as wives and mothers. These reports, Wolpe argues, ignored the reality of women's lives and the extent of their participation in the workforce. She discerns a contradiction between the ideology articulated in each of the reports about the need for education to suit individual capacities or abilities and their narrow prescriptions about education to prepare women for 'traditional' female roles.[16]

More recently, Deborah Thom complains that the Crowther Report, published in Britain in 1959, paid extensive attention to 'the inculcating of domesticity into all girls and to the recognition of their social role by the curriculum at secondary school', but failed to do so with regard to 'other factors of much moment in the lives of girls concerned'.[17] Her essay focuses particularly on the campaign for comprehensive schooling in Britain at this time and the attack on the selection tests for grammar schools, the 11+ examination. She sets out to show how, and then to explain why, the question of gender was not discussed to any significant extent in this campaign. This is, she suggests, a glaring omission, because 'After all, gender divisions are administratively organized, and can be seen with the naked eye, unlike those of class which rely on political insight or the work of a trained observer, a sociologist.'[18]

Thom, like Wolpe and Bland and her co-authors, fails to challenge the categories of men and women. Their concern with ideology is a concern with distorting images of women versus true or authentic ones. In criticizing documents like the Crowther Report for not recognizing or paying sufficient attention to the realities of girls' lives and experiences, this approach to feminist history contributes to the reifying of gendered categories rather than using history to destabilize them. They look to find where girls are spoken of as 'girls' in such documents, and find that the only place that they are discussed in these terms is where a specific set of capacities are talked of – those seen in this instance as necessary for the social roles of wife and mother. This is to assume that girls are only spoken of when they are referred to under the category of their sex; and it is to claim, similarly, that girls only find themselves spoken of and for when identified in this way. These analyses make the implicit supposition that other educational identities are not available to young women, that they cannot and do not understand themselves in a range of different ways. Instead of looking to investigate the historical and cultural determination of the terms of sexual difference, they assume its existence as somehow outside history and seek to show how it has been ignored or suppressed or distorted.

While not wanting to deny the significance of the times when girls were spoken about as defined first and foremost by their sex, I want to argue that other identities or subjectivities constituted in the educational and other discourses about young people of the 1950s and early 1960s did also address young women and in quite different forms. Official and popular rhetoric about adolescence, 'manpower needs', the 'wastage of talent', the 'need for a highly educated population in the new technological age' and 'citizens in the making', for instance, did not necessarily exclude girls.

I am not suggesting, however, that these discourses were (and are) not gendered. At an obvious level, educational literature, for instance, frequently used the pronoun 'he' or talked in terms of 'men'; at another level, it gave legitimacy also to notions of individual competitiveness and objective, rational thought which historically have been designated as masculine capacities and placed in opposition to characteristics such as cooperative and nurturing capacities designated as feminine. But neither of these points can be used to claim that young women found themselves necessarily excluded. To suggest that they do is to assume that young women are conscious of themselves at all times and in all places as gendered selves first and foremost and that they find themselves spoken to and for – interpellated – only as 'girls' or 'women'.

Carolyn Steedman's comments on the issue of the gendered character of our language are useful here. She challenges the assumption often made in contemporary equal opportunity literature that women in the past felt themselves necessarily shut out or invisible when the masculine pronoun was used in its universalizing form. 'It would seem', she says,

> that many women, living through the years of the 'sex-neutral "he"', refused, when they heard or used the pronoun to image a man. They thought rather of a genderless 'human being' or 'person'. Some of them, with much struggle, actually managed to image themselves – in the category of genderless human being.[19]

Similarly, I suggest, when girls in the 1950s saw only images of male scientists, encountered only male science teachers, or perceived that only values of objectivity, rationality, competitiveness, and even daring were affirmed in the academic curriculum, they did not necessarily immediately understand themselves – identify themselves – as sexed creatures, and hence, in these images, as of the wrong sex.[20] Certainly, as I will discuss in Chapter 7, there were new and powerful pressures in the 1950s to encourage young women to understand themselves as sexed through and through. But in looking at education, we need also to acknowledge the places where young women, by refusing or not recognizing the implicit or explicit masculinity of the images of educational achievement, found themselves spoken of and to in different ways.[21]

Histories of the schooling of girls, then, need to look at how such institutions are involved in the formation of complex and non-unified subjectivities. The girls' private schools of the 1950s, for instance, may have spoken to girls in terms of their being 'girls' through a range of practices – through instructions on deportment or the 'ladylike' way of wearing uniforms – but many of their educational policies and practices were preoccupied with the production of other capacities and ways of being in the world. Jill Ker Conway, recalling her schooling at Abbotsleigh in Sydney in the late 1940s and early 1950s, describes the strict requirements about dress, demeanour and speech required of 'young ladies' in the school, but she also writes of the stress on 'leadership', 'achievement' and 'the love of learning'. As a young woman at school and university, these latter educational vocabularies were central to her sense of herself and her future.[22] The practices and policies of schools focusing on such notions made available, albeit it more straightforwardly to a privileged minority of young women than to the mass of the population,[23] alternative forms of self-understanding – ways of constituting a self – to those which sought to form girls 'soaked in the immediate awareness of one's sex'.[24]

In writing a history of girlhood, then, we need to recognize how the interpellation of sexed subjects, as Teresa de Lauretis points out, does not occur in institutions like educational ones in a unitary way.[25] The construction of gender goes on busily in the daily life of schools, through a range of different processes. We need to study how such practices formulate and determine the terms of sexual difference in this setting, and the range of ways in which this is done.

As already indicated, the next two chapters explain the issues at stake in discussing what it means for women to grow up in the context of current feminist debates about the project of feminism. Both these chapters will discuss further the preoccupations which have shaped this book. Chapter 1 looks at how a number of contemporary positions in feminism understand its project as 'an awakening of women'. The assumptions about the growing up of women underlying each of these positions is questioned, as is the usefulness of this narrative of awakening to understanding the project of feminism today. Chapter 2 discusses the ways in which modern notions of the person and individuality have been defined in opposition to the feminine and what this means for women. Chapter 3 points to the way youth has been a key symbol in discussions of modernity, at the same time as the cultural ideal of the self-determining individual (seen as central to its project) has shaped contemporary understandings of what growing up – youth – is about. Chapters 4–7 use an account of the social definitions of girlhood and growing up in Australia in the 1950s and early 1960s to explore the historical relationship of women to the cultural ideals of personhood and individuality and to the understandings of growing up and maturity which these ideals have established as hegemonic in Western liberal democracies. On the basis of this history, I will suggest that feminists need to abandon notions of the project of feminism as being somehow about the growing up of women (however that is defined), at the same time as I look at why notions of 'growing up' have played such a powerful role in feminism.

1 // Feminism and the 'awakening of women'

The story of the awakening of women continues to hold considerable force in recent assessments of the past 20 or so years of feminism. Newspaper reports persist in speaking of feminism as 'women communicating with other women, encouraging them to break out *1990* of limiting stereotypes and to be a real person...'.[1] Sheila Rowbotham, in a more sustained analysis of the history of feminism since the 1960s, *The Past is Before Us* (1989), similarly writes of such a transformation. Her book records contemporary accounts by women of their involvement in the early stages of second-wave feminism. They speak very much in terms of their sense of awakening as they began to develop a shared sense of dissatisfactions. In her discussion of these narratives, Rowbotham, too, understands them as the 'stirrings of consciousness', the enabling of 'needs to emerge which had been ignored or dismissed within a well-defined concept of political, economic and social priorities', and 'the powerful longing to break out'.[2] Although she acknowledges that 'the "real" desires' of women may be 'more elusive than we had thought',[3] her narrative again is one of an awakening. She writes of women emerging into consciousness, out of silence into speech. Consciousness stirs, the real or authentic self longs to break the chains and flee from the invisible manacles that bind. Women awaken from an imposed condition of femininity to the so-called truth of their personhood.

In this history of feminism as an awakening, a central assumption is that of a set of capacities which define the person or individual as authentic, fulfilled, fully realized or fully human. Fundamental to these capacities is the need to determine one's own identity as an autonomous being. In the version of this story told by Friedan and others, the distorting and pacifying pleasures offered by the consumer culture of modern capitalism set out to persuade women to relinquish that fundamental and defining human need. That essential attribute of humanity emerges triumphant in the accounts of the flight from bondage, the stirrings of consciousness, the escape from repression. In her autobiography, *Taking it Like a Woman* (1984), Ann Oakley wrote of wanting to 'surpass her femininity'. The problem for women, she claims, is that:

> An autonomous sense of self, a self which exists outside and independently of relationships with others, does not need to develop; there are no factors which encourage it and many that militate against it. Women's sense of identity is thus dangerously bound up from early childhood with the identities of others.[4]

This particular story of the emergence of women from an imposed femininity, and the preoccupation with a particular formulation of the notion of the self-determining, autonomous individual which underlies it, has been rejected by a number of feminists and social theorists in recent years. Their reasons for doing so vary. The following two sections of this chapter examine two major feminist critiques of this ideal.

A pathology of women?

One line of feminist critique has sought to repudiate the model of human growth and development based upon this ideal of the self-determining, autonomous individual. In her book, *In a Different Voice* (1982), and in her more recent writings, Carol Gilligan provides one of the most powerful analyses of the supposed universality of this model of human development and its assumptions about the processes of identity formation. Focusing on the way in which this model operates in psychological literature, she argues that such theories do not accord with women's experience. But instead of attributing this disjunction to a problem of or in women themselves, as Betty Friedan had done, Gilligan insists that the literature itself is at fault. Women are not the developmental failures that Friedan claimed them to be. For Gilligan, the problem lies in the attempt by psychological theories to impose a definition of the essential attribute of humanity in the evaluation of women's lives which is simply not appropriate for them. The model of human growth, upon which these theories rely, refuses to listen to the voices of women and the very different stories they tell about their lives.

An image of the self in relationship, Gilligan claims, is characteristic of how women define themselves and their orientation to the

world. Rather than seeing relationships of dependence as impediments to the need to define an autonomous self, young women find
an alternative way. While psychology has traditionally cast the
problems of adolescence as the problem of separation (from parental
authority in particular), she suggests that the problem for young
women is instead one of conflicting loyalties:

> Seeking to perceive and respond to their own as well as to
> others' needs, adolescent girls ask if they can be responsive
> to themselves without losing connection with others and
> whether they can respond to others without abandoning
> themselves.[5]

This mode of making a self through the experience of relationships
with others and the acquiring of an understanding of and perspective on this experience of attachment, Gilligan insists, is not
a failure of self-definition, or individuation. It is an alternative way
of growing up. Prevailing interpretative schemes have failed to
reflect female experience and the way in which young women
have managed to resist, she claims, two long-standing equations:
'the equation of human with male and the equation of care with
self-sacrifice'. Though these schemes have celebrated selflessness as
the feminine virtue, young women have sought a different path in
which they have attempted to juggle loyalties to others' needs as
well as their own. The opposition between selfishness and selflessness so frequently posited in Western thought and literature has not
recognized, Gilligan contends, the way in which women have found
a way of imagining themselves as a self within the context of continuing relationships.[6]

The experience of young women in adolescence, Gilligan suggests, may help us to define a new vision of progress and civilization. In their finding an alternative way of defining the self, women
have recognized dependence as part of the human condition. But
dependence is not seen here as a position of powerlessness, of being
without control. On the contrary, Gilligan says, 'it signifies a conviction that one is able to have an effect on others, as well as the
recognition that the interdependence of attachment empowers both
the self and the other, not one at the other's expense'.[7]

Just as Friedan had seen herself in the 1960s as giving voice to the
stirrings of women's consciousness, to their dissatisfactions and slow
awakenings to their 'real' needs, Gilligan claimed 20 years later to
be opening up a space for women's authentic voices and desires
to be heard. In the latter account, however, they were to speak as
'women' and to insist on the legitimacy of their needs and desires
as such. Her writings call for attention to be paid to the experience

of adult life and growing up 'in women's own terms'.[8] As a feminist project, her work sets out to speak what she sees as 'the truth of women' and to give it space alongside the truth of men's development and adulthood. This too, then, is a story of awakening. It tells of women seeking to acknowledge their needs and desires, to fully realize their female self. In this account, women throw off the web of deceit that surrounds them and which proclaims their difference a lack or failure. They find their strength by turning towards each other and recognizing their common or shared life experience. And they insist upon public acceptance of their difference, an affirmation and valuing of the truth of women.

On the basis of the type of analysis provided by Gilligan, a number of feminist writers have set out to specify further the 'gender bias' in the models of human development and identity formation inherent in psychological and literary accounts of childhood and growing up. These studies seek to recover or constitute a female tradition of development in which the embeddedness seen as so central to the 'basic feminine sense of self'[9] no longer appears a failure of human growth or lack of person formation. The recognition and valuing of this tradition, it is claimed, constructs a picture of femininity as alternative, not inferior to masculinity.[10] Friedan's picture of the 'pathology' of women[11] in forfeiting the formation of themselves as autonomous is rejected, as are the concerns of the more contemporary feminists like Ann Oakley, for a different story of growing up – 'as a woman'.

In recent years, however, some feminists have attempted to go beyond accusations of gender blindness or bias in the dominant models of human development. This project undertakes a thorough-going critique and reconstruction of the categories so central to this model. Joining with other strands of thought in social theory which have begun to challenge and re-work 'the fundamental categories, methodology and self-understanding of western science and theory',[12] this critique has begun to re-examine concepts like those of the individual, the self and essential human attributes. This development in feminist thought refuses to leave the prevailing notions intact by simply asserting a different truth for women. While building on the criticisms of the normative models of human growth and maturity initiated by feminists such as Gilligan, it has attempted to take her work further to reassess in fundamental ways the concepts underlying those models and the cultural and political ideals they express.

Although Gilligan claims to look at the sociological uniqueness of women's experience of the modern world, her search for 'the truth of women', for the different voice, undermines her declared project of providing a 'complex rendition of human experience'.[13] Her search for a feminine self as an alternative to the masculine notions of the self as one which is to be found in texts as diverse as nineteenth-century novels, like George Eliot's *Mill on the Floss* (1860), and interviews with contemporary young women, ignores historical questions of the transformations constantly taking place in the construction of female subjectivities. She provides a powerful argument for the need for a different sense of self and an alternative ethic of caring and responsibility for others than those currently dominant in contemporary Western culture, but she does not investigate questions of the historical and changing nature of subjectivities. In claiming to speak 'the truth of women', her work is in danger of establishing its own normative model of how women should grow up against which at least some women will be found, once again, to be 'developmental failures'.[14]

In the following section, I draw on aspects of developments in recent feminist and other social theory which point to the necessity of taking a more historical approach to the question of the constitution of female subjectivities. This work has questioned the fundamental categories of the individual and the self, as well as the dichotomy constituted between the individual and the social which has been so central to the development of the human sciences in the twentieth century.

Authentic selves

In the stories of 'awakening' told of the origins and purpose of second-wave feminism, women find either their authentic individual or female selves by throwing off the shackles and myths of the social world that surrounds them. Underlying this notion of liberation is an assumption about the separateness of the 'individual' and the 'social' which has been criticized from a number of different perspectives. In the Friedan-type account, a concept of human essence is at work which suggests that the problem for women is that this essence has been continually repressed or stunted by social conditions. Forces like the mass media or the advertising industry have prevented its development or full realization in women. In Gilligan's alternative story of women 'choosing' themselves, the category of women, as Adams and Minson have argued, is another version of this notion of a human essence. '"Women" marks the always given gender in the category of humanity, a gender to which essential truths are ascribed.'[15] According to the narrative provided in this instance, the bias in models of human growth fails to give public recognition to those attributes; the awakening of women facilitates their own recognition and embracing of that female self as one shared by all women and the throwing off of the social restraints – the male bias in the models of human growth – which have inhibited their full enjoyment of those capacities.[16] In both accounts, then, the social constrains the individual and liberation requires its removal or rejection.

As Henriques and his co-authors have noted in their critique of psychological knowledges, this notion of liberation carries with it the belief that the individual can be free from social restraints and 'be a pure and untainted entity'.[17] Their work develops an alternative perspective through an analysis of the way in which concepts of 'the individual' and 'the society' are products of the knowledges and practices of institutions concerned with the regulation of the social world. Rather than individuality being a possession of the pre-social or ahistorical individual, these authors argue that our modern forms of individuality are historical products. The attributes of the individual considered as defining of the human essence are, thus, capacities produced in the modern individual rather than natural or pre-social endowments. The competency and the desire to take responsibility for one's own actions in specific situations result from a set of trainings of the individual rather than from the maturation of certain pre-existing human potentials of that individual. Similarly, the need and the ability to define oneself or determine one's own identity are not qualities of the pre-social individual, but attributes produced in definite social arrangements. They are the result of particular socio-historical formations, rather than natural features of our humanness. As John Grumley argues:

> Even if some capacities seem so fundamental to our very humanness that it would be difficult to contemplate life without them, this must be recognized for what it is as a choice which ascribes a historically formed quality the status of 'nature'.[18]

These seemingly natural and indisputable needs and competencies are social characteristics just as are other capacities commonly understood as the result of socialization.

The production of individuals 'free to choose' is, then, a cultural requirement. As Jeffrey Minson has argued:

> the modern category of the human person entails a capacity to make certain (orderly) choices, to initiate certain actions and to resist certain sorts of regulations. The question is, how

have these capacities been constructed – and in relation to what?[19]

These capacities to choose are produced through a range of institutional practices and associated forms of expertise. Participating in these institutional practices accustoms and trains individuals to act, think and desire according to particular sets of rules or norms. They incite in individuals both an orientation to and the wish to transform themselves according to those rules and thereby to seek to attain a certain state of human 'happiness, purity, wisdom, perfection, or immortality'.[20] The 'self-determining individual' is a notion of an individual who has learnt to employ these 'technologies of the self', as Foucault calls them,[21] to act upon his or her self, to produce the self in this form. Modern individuals, according to this notion, have a sense both of their capacity to choose – to govern their own lives – and the pleasures involved in, as well as the social obligation for them to do so. Taking responsibility for one's self, understanding oneself as making choices and determining one's own life, is a matter of learning particular techniques of acting on the self and of constituting the self as one's own project. These needs and abilities, to reiterate the point already made, are not qualities of the pre-social individual allowed to flourish or to be crushed by particular social arrangements. They are cultural characteristics produced in particular socio-historical formations.

A number of feminist writers, however, have questioned the way the notion of the autonomous, self-defining individual has been understood from a different angle. They, too, recognize that this concept describes a cultural ideal encountered in particular historical and social institutions, but they use this insight to call for a critique of that ideal and associated notions of the self and identity central to traditions of Western political thought. Building on the work of writers like Carol Gilligan, who have pointed to the sociological uniqueness of women's experience of social relations in the modern world, they argue that different concepts of the self and identity can and need to be generated which recognize and value those different experiences.

Carole Pateman, for instance, has analysed the way in which the concept of the individual in liberal democratic discourses abstracts individuals from their group membership and ascribed characteristics. Political programmes of equal opportunity, such as those operating in contemporary governmental policies about equal opportunity for girls and women in education, tend to work within this framework. These programmes conceptualize the problem as one of the effects of the social on the individual. Social characteristics such as gender, race and class membership are seen as separate from and contingent to the individual. They are burdens or encumbrances to be removed from the individual under the influence of a good education. Freed from the impact of these social factors, which are seen as non-essential to what the individual really is, she will be able to develop her own capacities and become a fully autonomous being.[22]

Yet, within this equal opportunity framework, it is only women who appear to be burdened by the social. Men's activities, attitudes, choices and characteristics represent the norm against which women are judged as lacking or constrained by the social. The uninterrogated concept of the autonomous, self-defining individual is implicitly gendered. Independence and autonomy, the rational mind freed from the distorting effects of the emotions and the needs of the body, and the individual unrestrained by private or domestic responsibilities able to devote all his energies to public activities, represent values and characteristics historically associated with the masculine. But, perhaps more importantly, they have also achieved their meaning and status by establishing a series of negations which have been at one and the same time identified with the feminine. As Seyla Benhabib argues, women have become associated in Western political and moral theory with what men are not:

> namely, they are not autonomous, independent, but by the same token, non-aggressive but nurturant, not competitive but giving, not public but private. The world of the female is constituted by a series of negations. She is simply what he happens not to be.[23]

But, unlike Gilligan, Benhabib does not remain preoccupied with giving voice and recognition to those repressed values with which women have historically been associated.[24] She proposes instead a fundamental reassessment of our concepts of individuality and humanity. Her argument is similar to the one put forward by Henriques *et al.* and others, which suggests that our individuality lies not in some pre-social self or human essence which must free itself from the social world and social relations in which we live to be fully realized. The self is neither disembodied nor unencumbered by social relations. Rather, our individuality is produced precisely by the way in which our experiences of embodiment have been socially constructed, as well as, more generally, by the particular social and historical arrangements in which we live. The uniqueness of the self is not to be found by 'driving a wedge' between the self and its social role, but in recognizing 'the plurality of diverse selves', as Pauline Johnson explains, produced by a highly diverse modern culture.[25]

New identities

In the light of these moves to rethink fundamental concepts of the individual, the self and identity formation, how then should we understand the stories of awakening operating in various accounts of the emergence and project of second-wave feminism? They claim to be revealing an already given identity – whether of the modern individual awaiting the opportunity to be fully realized or of a female self seeking public recognition, a position from which to speak and to be heard. These accounts, I suggest instead, are implicated in the *construction* of a public form of identification, a means of understanding one's place in the world and the way in which one can and should act in that world as a political agent. Their role is to produce meaning rather than simply to communicate it.[26]

To take the two forms of this genre separately: The workings of the Betty Friedan-type story can be seen most clearly in the accounts provided by women of their own awakening as recorded, for example, by Ann Oakley. When writing of their own awakening, feminist writers construct an autobiographical narrative in which they 'come to realize' that the roles of wife and mother restrict their freedom and their power to define their own identities. Often through participating in the confessional space of a women's consciousness-raising group, they begin to recognize and articulate their dissatisfaction with these roles and to learn to speak of a different sense of self. The credibility and legitimacy of the search for such a self is understood as guaranteed by the concepts of the fully formed, self-defining individual. However, as Rita Felski argues in her discussion of the confessional mode in feminist autobiographies, this process of writing about the self involves the production of a normative definition of subjectivity. Drawing on Michel Foucault's work on the history of sexuality, she points to the way in which this genre participates in a well-established tradition in Western culture of confessional practices in which the individual is brought not to recognize but to constitute him or herself as a specific type of subject. These practices produce a form of subjectivity – particular desires and needs – rather than liberate pre-existing desires and needs. The individual learns to understand him or herself as having these desires and needs and as having a responsibility or need to speak of them. Feminist autobiographies as public documents are similarly actively involved in the creation of a symbolic or cultural identity. This identity is one in which the individual participates in practices which define the self as autonomous, as separate from social relationships. It involves a normative definition of subjectivity which requires the individual to take personal responsibility for one's own life and self-definition. This version of the feminist confession genre provides exemplary accounts of such practices of the self.

In the story of awakening told by Gilligan, on the other hand, she writes of the voices of women silenced by the knowledge and conventions of behavioural scientists. She attempts to give public space to the authentic voices of women and to give affirmation to their need for self-recognition. In claiming to facilitate the legitimation of the 'truth of women', Gilligan is contributing to a narrative of female self-discovery and self-validation which constructs an oppositional female public identity. Yet, certain representations of this female self tend to ignore or fail to recognize that this identity is a social construction and talk in terms of an essential or authentic feminine self gaining public recognition or expression. Feminism is represented as being about women as a group finding an authentic sense of self; one that is autonomous, self-defined.[27] But as Felski reminds us, such rhetoric is involved in the constitution of women as a specific cultural identity at a particular historical moment, rather than giving an appropriate and proper voice to an already existing, or potentially existing, identity. It works towards establishing such an identity – of women speaking as 'women' – as a publicly available one and as an active political force at a particular point in time. Such representations incite the desire to be heard, to intervene or take action in the public sphere of political debate and policy decisions, in forms which were both politically effective and felt to be meaningful by at least certain individuals.

I am suggesting, then, that both stories of awakening need to be understood as specific political strategies devised at particular points in history. Both provide forms of public identification which constitute women as a group seeking to be heard and to be recognized as political agents. Their force lies not in any liberation or awakening of women, but in their creation of new political identities, public forms of identification, which constitute women as active political agents in different ways (and mostly at different points in time). The disparity, on the other hand, between these two accounts of the project and emergence of second-wave feminism, can be explained in terms of the inevitable uncertainties and oscillations which Denise Riley argues lie at the core of the history of feminism. She suggests that the constant shifts in the arguments of feminists between seeking a space for women to speak as 'women' or laying claim to their recognition within such general categories as seemingly gender-neutral individuals or persons should not be cause for despair. She explains:

> Feminism has intermittently been as vexed with the urgency
> of disengaging from the category 'women' as it has with laying

claim to it; twentieth-century European feminism has been constitutionally torn between fighting against over-feminisation and against under-feminisation, especially where social policies are at stake.[28]

The two stories of awakening I have focused on here can, then, be seen as different strategies in the struggle against how women have been positioned as 'women'. Betty Friedan sought to constitute an alternative public identification for women than the one that she saw as dominant in the USA in the 1950s. Carol Gilligan, on the other hand, set out to represent women as a unity through her claims for a different 'truth of women' in opposition to a behavioural science which in the name of the 'individual' obliterated the concrete specificity of people's lives. Gilligan fights against the under-feminization of women; Betty Friedan was fighting against their over-feminization.

To seek only to explain the disparity between these two stories of awakening in terms of a difference in tactics is, however, unsatis-factory. Such an analysis would fail to confront the question of the project of feminism today. Denise Riley's book is a powerful account of the necessary impossibility of this project establishing for all time a set of shared and constant values and understandings – of the way in which, in Meaghan Morris's terms, the very concept of a 'project' requires that those values remain 'undecided and unsettled'.[29] But it is necessary to make some assessment of the usefulness of the dif-ferent strategies at different points in time. In this book, I will show how second-wave feminism emerged at a time when women were being constituted as a unified group in powerful ways. The taking up of this identification 'women' by feminism in its seeking to speak to and for 'women' made sense for a while at least. The social definition of women as a group with shared needs and life experi-ences was a central force in creating the conditions for the emergence of a new social subject – 'women who want to speak and take political action as "women"'. But we need to recognize the historical specificity of that moment for feminism, and its restrictions for feminism in the 1990s. While the identification 'women' continues to mobilize some women in this form today, major changes have occurred in the forms of public identification which are socially available and seen as desirable, which limit the extent to which all women can, or would want to, understand themselves in this form. Feminism itself has played a major role in these changes. In fighting against the 'over-feminization' of women, it has been successful in challenging the extent to which young women today need to understand themselves 'as first and foremost' sexed identities. This,

ironically, at the same time, has limited the extent to which feminism can call out to them as identifying themselves as 'women' who
would want to speak and take action in the world in this form.

The problem for feminism is not, however, to find, in a once and
for all way, how all women can find themselves properly spoken for
as 'women'. The problem for feminism is, I suggest, more mundane
and, yet, simultaneously more radical. First, we need to continue
to refuse all attempts to 'pin us to our sex'[30] – the claims made by
particular uses of the category 'women' to speak the truth of us.
Second, we need, also, to question our desires to find a home or
'safe places', as Biddy Martin and Chandra Mohanty call them, within
such identifications as 'women' or 'feminists'.[31] That is, we need
to be wary of the way in which feminism itself can be involved in
strengthening rather than destabilizing the category 'woman'. And,
third, we need to continue to take up those issues where we have
to speak 'as women' in order to point to and fight against the
conditions and assumptions which have produced problems of dis-
advantage and suffering for those identified in this form – as 'women'.
These three points summarize, I suggest, the activities of feminists
today; the radicalness, I referred to, lies in the ambition to undertake all three tasks at once.

In this chapter, I have examined two different accounts of feminism
and the ways in which they can be seen to have conceptualized
its project in terms of an awakening of women. I have suggested
that rather than simply facilitating that process, as they have claimed
for themselves, their texts have instead been involved in the production of a new social subject. Rather than liberating already existing selves from the social constraints which surround them, these
public forms of identification have provided new selves with corres-
ponding new needs and desires – needs and desires, in particular, to
act politically and to seek to be heard. Why these stories of awakening
'work', why they do get taken up by individual women as powerful
forms of self-understanding and why they have succeeded in constituting women as a political force at particular points in time represents a different set of questions. This study cannot address all
these issues. It does go some way, however, towards exploring the
second of these questions in looking at at least some of the conditions
which made possible the emergence of second-wave feminism; that
is, the conditions which made it possible for the emergence of a
new social subject of women as a group demanding to be heard and
to act politically in Australia in the late 1960s and early 1970s.

But the point I wish to make at this stage is that, whatever else
the project of feminism is about, it is not about the growing up of

women as a group. The 'problem' for feminism is not about women realizing or finding either their authentic individual selves or female selves. Both accounts of the project of feminism looked at in this chapter relied on or sought to establish a cultural ideal of what it means for women to grow up. This book investigates why feminism has been conceptualized in these terms, just as it seeks to understand why the question of 'am I grown up yet?' continues to be a powerful one for women who grew up in the 1950s and 1960s.

2 /// The importance of having: modernity, women and consumerism

In her analysis of 'the feminine mystique', Betty Friedan blamed the consumer society for persuading women to forfeit their personhood. Modern forms of advertising, she said, set out to sell women false promises of identity and individuality. Her argument ensured that the place of modern popular culture in women's lives would be central to feminist agendas in the following decades. But her claims about women's failure to grow up also continued a more established tradition of constituting personhood as opposed to womanhood. It was this tradition which Gilligan sought to challenge in identifying an alternative definition of adulthood for women. In this chapter, I examine a number of the key debates about cultural moderniz-ation to explore further how the opposition between womanhood and personhood has been constituted. I begin by examining the tradition of cultural critique to which Friedan contributed, a tradition in which women are characteristically portrayed as the victims of the processes of modernization. I look at one paradigmatic diagnosis of modernity to outline the context in which the figure of 'woman' is employed to articulate a profound ambivalence about those features of the contemporary social world said to be central to its modernity. Next, I discuss an apparently alternative tradition of celebrating women's enjoyment of popular culture and the processes of cultural modernization and argue that it fails to break with the ideal of personhood established by the first tradition's representation of women as the victims of modernization. Finally, I look at the suggestion that both these traditions of cultural analysis have not engaged sufficiently with the particularity of women's experience of modernity. I argue that an account of the specific contexts in which women encounter concrete formulations of the cultural ideals of personhood and individuality will reveal both the problems and the possibilities thereby opened up for women by this ideal at any historical moment.

Modernity

David Frisby has pointed to the significance of Marshall Berman's book, *All that is Solid Melts into Air* (1985), as one of the key texts in making the theme of modernity central once again to discussions of social theory.[1] In this book, Berman elaborates an analysis of modernity as a set of social and economic conditions and as a cultural project. It is a vivid and rich piece of writing and is paradigmatic for its explanation of what is at stake in talking of contemporary social conditions in terms of their 'modernity'. He sets out to recover, and constitute, a tradition of critical engagement with these conditions, a tradition he labels 'modernist'. I use Berman here for the clarity of his insights into what is meant by modernity in a whole range of settings. I draw on aspects of his analysis at various stages in this book. I also wish to point, however, to his failure to acknowledge how women are defined in the cultural critiques he seeks to celebrate.[2]

Berman describes modernity as first and foremost a body of experiences:

> To be modern . . . is to experience personal and social life as a maelstrom, to find one's world and oneself in perpetual disintegration and renewal, trouble and anguish, ambiguity and contradiction: to be part of a universe in which all that is solid melts into air.[3]

He refers to the social processes that have brought this maelstrom into being, and continually renew its conditions of existence, as the forces of modernization. These processes include immense demographical upheavals; industrialization; rapid and often cataclysmic urban growth; the emergence and continual expansion of the systems of mass communication; the capitalist world market and its drastic and continual fluctuations.[4] Modernization continually brings about major transformations in the broad social, economic and political structures of our time, as well as in the everyday world of people's lives.

The main focus of Berman's study is a group of writers and a range of social movements which he characterizes as modernist. The visions articulated in various contexts that can be described in this way, he argues, all share the desire to 'make men and women the subjects as well as the objects of modernization'.[5] Writers in this modernist tradition set out to engage critically with these processes, to confront the forces which continually threaten to overcome us, but to do so in terms which enable us to embrace the opportunities offered in this world of continual change for 'the open-ended development of self and society'.[6] Berman commends both the critical spirit and, as he sees it, the optimism of modernism. With a characteristic flourish, he describes modernity as a project in the following terms:

> To be a modern*ist* is to make oneself somehow at home in the maelstrom, to make its rhythms one's own, to move within its currents in search of the forms of reality, of beauty, of freedom, of justice, that its fervid and perilous flow allows.[7]

The cultural project of modernity, says Berman, is to 'heal the wounds of modernity' by seeking a 'fuller and deeper modernity'. The image of the good life for the modernist is not 'a life of definitive perfection', it is a life of 'continual, restless, open-ended unbounded growth'.[8]

According to Berman, those who share this vision, and articulated it in the past with great force, included Goethe, Marx and Baudelaire. In more recent times, he identifies a divergent set of materials as evidence of the continuing interest in and vitality of this modernist project (though he notes, too, its increasing problems in the decades after the Second World War). He points to the writings of Paul Goodman on the dilemmas of youth in the post-Second World War era, the films of Jean-Luc Godard, the 1960s songs of Bob Dylan, the street protests of the 1960s, and the ecological movements of the 1970s and 1980s concerned with recycling and urban renewal. These cultural critics and cultural forms have attempted to engage fully with the contingency of human existence with which modernity confronts men and women, as well as the conditions of freedom it simultaneously offers.

The figure of Faust, Berman argues, has long been one of the major heroes of modern culture. His story continues to be told or alluded to in contemporary settings with fascination and fear; an intellectual non-conformist with a powerful mind and grand-scale visions of modernization, he is also the scientist who loses control of the products of his imagination and intellectual energies. Berman uses Goethe's exploration of the Faust legend as a key text in order to spell out the main themes of his book. In *Faust*, Goethe celebrates large-scale modernization projects designed to transform society's productive forces for the long-term benefit of all. Such projects seek to make people masters of their own destinies – in control of their own fates, rather than subject to the whims of nature or the dictates of tradition. Immense construction projects such as the building of dams or transportation systems like railways, canals or highways typify such ' "Faustian models" of development' in Berman's terms. It is only in the twentieth century, he suggests, that this model has come into its own:

> In the capitalist world it has emerged most vividly in the proliferation of 'public authorities' and superagencies designed to organize immense construction projects, especially in transportation and energy: canals and railroads, bridges and highways, dams and irrigation systems, hydroelectric power plants, nuclear reactors, new towns and cities, the exploration of outer space.[9]

But Goethe also warns of the forces potentially unleashed by such projects. Faust is both a heroic and tragic figure. He envisages a world in which the personal growth of the individual goes hand in hand with economic and social progress. Yet he refuses to see and to take responsibility for the potential human costs of his visions. In this 'tragedy of development', an old couple – Philemon and Baucis – and the female figure of Gretchen are the victims of modernization. Represented as inhabitants of the 'closed social world' of the traditional small town, they symbolize all that is best of that old world and of the human values potentially and irrevocably sacrificed to the processes of modernization.

Berman fails to acknowledge that the use of a female figure to represent the Other of modernity – the closed individual of the traditional world and the victim of the human costs and tragedy of modernization – is typical of modernist writings. Yet this has become a major point of criticism of modernist texts in recent years. Meaghan Morris, for instance, in her discussion of suburban shopping centres, argues that feminists must be alert to the dangers of the way in which various cultural critics have sought to articulate a profound ambivalence about modernization processes through allegorical female figures. She asks the question 'how do classical theories of modernism fall short of women's modernity?'[10] Pointing to the way in which the home, and hence women's lives, has long been one of the major experimental sites of modernization, she challenges the inability of theorists of the modern, like Walter Benjamin and Terry Eagleton, to deal with changes in the spheres of cultural production in modern society and, more particularly, with the changing nature of women's relationship to modernity.

This issue has been discussed at greater length by Andreas Huyssen. He analyses literary texts such as Gustave Flaubert's *Madame Bovary*, as well as the cultural criticism of writers like Theodor Adorno and Siegfried Kracauer. These writers are all characterized as modernist by Huyssen. He examines the way in which each expresses their ambivalence about the impact of modernization in the realm of cultural production by representing mass culture as the 'Other' through the gendering of its products and its consumers. *Madame Bovary*, according to Huyssen, is the classic example of how modernist texts have frequently drawn these connections quite explicitly. Emma Bovary is the passive victim of the products of modern cultural technologies – of the printing press and, in particular, of the mass circulation of pulp romance novels. High culture is implicitly understood in Flaubert's text as the privileged site of male activities; only a female figure could fall prey to the false promises and inauthentic needs created by mass culture.

Franco Moretti, in his book *The Way of the World* (1987), also focuses on Flaubert's *Madame Bovary* as a key modernist text. His analysis makes clearer what is at stake for Flaubert in his description of Emma's consumption of mass culture and voracious desire for commodities. Emma avidly reads the popular novels of her time, filling her head with destructive fantasies and desires. She desperately seeks to transform her life and to set herself free from the traditional norms and rules which surround her to become a modern individual; but she sets out to do so, not by her own actions or by attempting to determine her own identity. She believes that she can do so, rather, by buying – by avid commodity consumption. According to Moretti, Flaubert was the first novelist to narrate what he saw as 'the tragedy of the consumer'. Flaubert sets out to demonstrate the falsity and destructiveness of the notion that simply through 'having' one can 'put aside one's "being" and forge a new one'.[11] He portrays Emma Bovary as failing to recognize the necessity for the individual in the modern world to take responsibility for defining one's self, for accepting the burdens and the pleasures of becoming self-legislating through one's own actions or achievements. Emma forfeits her claims to personhood. She falls victim to the products she consumes and, in the end, she destroys herself and her family.

In his discussion of the writings of cultural critics like Adorno and Kracauer, Huyssen suggests that modernist writers explore their ambivalence about mass culture and its consumers – the masses – through the use of gendered language as well as through constituting more explicit associations with the feminine. 'The fear of the masses', he says, 'is always also a fear of woman, a fear of nature out of control, a fear of the unconscious, of sexuality, of the loss of identity and stable ego boundaries.'[12] Modernism, in these terms, claims to require a clear set of boundaries between itself and mass culture in order to maintain its adversary stance both towards the products of bourgeois culture and the everyday life of that society.

According to Andreas Huyssen, the dichotomy which depicts mass culture as engulfing, totalitarian and feminine, and modernism as progressive, dynamic and indicative of male cultural superiority, has been challenged practically and theoretically for some time now. He points to those arguments made in the name of the post-modern which attempt to undermine and reject that dichotomy and to the particular role of a feminist critique in this context. Though he acknowledges that 'the ideology of modernism' continues to occupy major positions of authority in cultural institutions such as the museum or the academy, it is, he announces, 'a thing of the past'.[13] I wish, however, to point to the way the dichotomies constituted in modernism between passivity and activity, agent and victim, subject and object, have not been abandoned in feminist writings about the processes of cultural modernization. In the following section, I examine the way studies of women's consumption of popular culture have not departed in any significant manner from the notion of personhood employed by Flaubert in his account of 'the tragedy of the consumer'.

Women, mass culture and consumerism

In a number of recent important papers on consumerism, Mica Nava argues that the relative status and power of women has paradoxically been enhanced by the consumer society of modern capitalism. Consumption, she asserts, 'has offered women new areas of authority and expertise, new sources of income, a new sense of consumer rights . . .'.[14] To support her claim, she refers briefly to the work of Donzelot, who suggests that the delineation of the modern family as a private space by various governmental bodies involved the creation of new competencies and responsibilities in women – the creation of new forms of agency for women or new subject positions for them to occupy. Donzelot's analysis cuts across feminist histories which have seen the formation of the modern family as securing the oppression of women and their subordination to men. He argues that this process of modernization should not be understood within a framework which seeks to point out yet another instance of the repression of women. He sets out to show how it created new forms of subjectivities or social agency. Women were provided with new responsibilities and powers, and the transformation of the family, effected by the intervention of various professional groups, was secured through the active participation of women.[15]

Similarly, then, Nava proposes that we understand the rise of the consumer society as entailing the production of new capacities and skills in women – a set of responsibilities and a range of powers which were represented at least up until recent years as feminine. The implication of her argument here is that consumerism requires the creation of new forms of social agency or new subjectivities, rather than the repression, crushing or deformation of a pre-existing, pre-social agent. But Nava attempts to retain notions of subversion and resistance, which sit uneasily with her analysis in this instance. She claims to take her concept from Foucault. Foucault, she says, insisted that wherever there is power 'there is the potential for its resistance'.[16] Yet, she seems unclear about how this resistance occurs. Her problem here is no doubt in part due to Foucault's own frequent lack of clarity on this issue – he makes but fleeting references to the notion of resistance. It is nevertheless a significant aspect of Nava's argument and reveals a fundamental problem which her analysis has failed to confront. Her reference to 'potential' for resistance, as well as her wish to look for the 'chances of subversion',[17] suggest that she retains a notion of a pre-existing agent, a subjectivity which can stand outside or apart from social relations and which has a predilection to resist or subvert power relations. She asserts that notions of agency and resistance must be taken seriously, but does not explain sufficiently what she means by these terms.[18]

Concepts of resistance and subversion have had an important history in studies of popular culture since the Second World War. Emerging in part out of reactions to particular forms of Marxist analyses of the processes by which social and cultural order are maintained, they served, among other purposes, to reject notions of false consciousness. The masses were not, it was claimed, to be seen any longer as dupes, victims only of manipulation and the distorted views of the world propagated by the new culture industries. This argument sought to break down the distinction between the consumers of popular culture and high culture, and hence to reject one of the dichotomies fundamental to the modernist traditions. In studies of youth culture initiated by the Birmingham Centre for Contemporary Cultural Studies, the notion of resistance was employed to suggest that the apparent consumerism of post-war youth was not to be understood as demonstrating their readiness to be manipulated by the new consumer industries directed at the youth market, and to argue that this consumerism should not be read as evidence of the disappearance of class. The use of the commodities such as clothes, popular music and other items by particular groups of young people in the development of subcultural styles constituted, they argued, 'resistance through rituals'.[19] The purpose of the concept of resistance in such analyses was to demonstrate the agency of subordinated groups, their refusal to be defined and dominated by the powerful groups in society. It sought, thus, to break with the way in which the masses had been conceptualized in so many modernist texts as 'Other'.

It is not surprising, then, that feminist studies of women and popular culture have retained this concept as a way of making a claim for the agency of women against their construction as passive and gullible: a conception which, as we have seen, has provided such a powerful and convenient image in the modernist critique of cultural modernization. Studies of soap opera or romance stories, in particular, which have argued for the necessity of looking at the progressive features of these popular culture forms and the pleasures women gain from them, work within this resistance framework. Janice Radway, for instance, in an important study conducted in the early 1980s, discussed romance fiction as allowing women to cope with the drudgery of their daily lives, but, at the same time, she pointed to the pleasure which women found in these stories as evidence of both their hopes for a better life as well as their resistance to the seeming inevitability of their social conditions.[20]

Similarly, many of the essays in a collection edited by Mary Ellen Brown, *Television and Women's Culture* (1990), use concepts of resistance and subversion to represent women as actively choosing – agents rather than victims – enjoying the products of mass culture for their own ends. John Fiske, one of the authors, insists that women are neither 'complicit in, nor do they find pleasure in, their subordination under patriarchy'. Writing about the place of contemporary television quiz shows in what he refers to as 'women's culture', he comments: 'If quiz shows are popular with women (and they are), they are so only because they bear not only the ideological voices of the dominant, but also the opportunity to resist, evade or negotiate with these voices.'[21] Popular culture, he argues, is a matter of what people make do with in their everyday lives – in particular, of what they do with the mass cultural products provided for them. Mary Ellen Brown concludes the collection of essays with a claim that the act of consumption should be understood as political in so far as women 'nominate, value, and regulate their own pleasure'.[22] She hopes to demonstrate the 'strengths of women', the way in which their subordinate position in the social and economic order does not simply make them victims.

Yet these arguments about resistance leave intact many of the dichotomies seen as problematic in modernist traditions of cultural critique. Most notably, they do not seek to abandon the oppositions between active versus passive, subject versus object, agent versus victim, independent versus dependent. They contrive instead to show that the consumers of popular culture can be characterized as demonstrating the characteristics deemed most desirable by each of these dichotomies constituted by modernism. And, perhaps most ironically, in the studies of popular culture and women, the dichotomy masculine versus feminine is also retained by the way in which these studies talk of the oppression of women, women's culture and the resistance of women. That is, 'women' become an always-already-constituted group, a group whose shared characteristics are assumed to be somehow pre-existing the forms in which they are addressed by mass culture. According to this type of analysis, women respond as a group because they are somehow necessarily already one; they have shared interests in television programmes because they already necessarily have common desires and needs for pleasure.

Concepts of the resisting or actively choosing subject which continue to preoccupy studies of popular culture remain trapped within notions of the pre-social individual. They hunt out evidence of the pre-existing, choosing agent, the subjectivity which is either to be crushed by or to stand up to social forces. This insistence on the resisting or active subject may demonstrate that the cultural critic refuses to be patronizing about popular culture and its consumers, but, in terms of its politics, it takes us no further than a vision of embattled selves in a harsh world 'making do'. Here I tend to be sympathetic to Judith Williamson's irritation with academic studies of popular culture 'busy picking out strands of "subversion" ', withdrawing from any exercise of critical judgement of the products of mass culture themselves or concrete considerations of how social change might be effected.[23]

My reasons for rejecting the notions of resistance and subversion are, nevertheless, at least initially, different. My central concern here, as already indicated, is the way in which this approach to the issue of women and popular culture retains the dichotomies established by modernism and, in particular, the dichotomy between the categories of personhood and woman. Women, according to the framework used in these analyses of popular culture, may now be recognized as both persons and women – rather than simply the forfeited selves of Betty Friedan's analysis – but the distinction remains. As resisting subjects, they are now accorded the status of persons because they are self-defining or choosing individuals as demonstrated through their apparent inclination to resist or subvert any attempts to dominate them; but in their tastes in popular culture and in their constitution as a unified group who are studied as pre-existing in this form, they reveal their Otherness, their womanhood (even if that status is now deemed acceptable).

If, however, we understand the capacities and desires for self-determination – represented by the notion of resistance and associated concepts as pre-social – to be, instead, qualities produced within particular socio-historical formations in modern individuals, as I argued in Chapter 1, then these dichotomies can be broken down. Such an approach requires a framework which is far more historically specific and contextual in its judgements about and accounts of the relationship of women to the products of modernization – such as mass culture – as well as to the cultural ideals of personhood and individuality. Though Nava's analysis points in this direction, retaining the categories of resistance and subversion prevents her from pursuing an orientation which is sufficiently historical. Rather than looking always for resistance, subversion, or even containment, we need to look at the historical and changing relationship of women to modern cultural ideals, as well as to the changing purposes, and hence contingent nature, of our own judgements of what is at stake at any particular moment in talking of the issues raised by Flaubert's 'tragedy of the consumer'.

Women and modernity

In her analysis of the cultural criticism produced in Weimar Germany, Patrice Petro has provided one such historical account of women's relationship to modernity. She argues that the reasons why mass culture was symbolized as feminine in the work of critics like Benjamin and Kracauer cannot simply be reduced to their participation in the modernist tradition of constituting the feminine as Other. They also constantly drew connections between mass culture and the feminine, she claims, because they recognized the way in which its products did precisely give a new social space and public visibility to women. Her study looks at how these writers, despite their ambivalence about what they constituted as the feminine, were documenting the production of historically unprecedented modes of consumption, identification and subjectivity. Through their focus on the historical and changing nature of subjectivity, they were breaking down some of the central dichotomies of modernism, such as the distinction between activity and passivity. Their work revealed how women in 1920s Germany were crucial to the processes of modernization as labour (in terms of the sorts of occupations they were taking up) and as consumers – creating and being created as a new demand for new forms of technologies and new forms of cultural goods. Benjamin and Kracauer attempted to investigate the new forms of subjectivity produced by the major changes occurring in domains such as those of the technologies of cultural production, the organization of work and the social relations of the modern city.[24]

Thus, Petro's reading of the work of these cultural critics suggests that we need to look at the relationship of women to modernity in historically specific ways. For instance, in studying women's relationship to the products and the technologies of cultural modernization, concepts like resistance and false consciousness prevent us from asking questions about the historically profound effects which not just the contents of these cultural products but the technologies involved in their dissemination have on the subjectivities made available to women and on their experiences of modernity. In undertaking this work we can then ask specific questions about the political consequences of the changes thus brought about. This will mean, too, that we will move away from relying (as the resistance framework does) on a vague and unexamined sense of dark times and the need to look for signs of hopes or points of vulnerability in the system which we assume always remains the same. We will need instead to be explicit about the specific contemporary concerns we are addressing and the way in which our analyses seek to address those concerns.

In this study, I am investigating how modern notions of personhood and individuality began to be understood as forms of identification culturally available to and socially desirable for women. These ideals are never encountered in abstract form. In the following chapter, I begin to look at how they were interpreted or translated in various contexts into modern notions about youth and normative definitions of growing up in the 1950s and 1960s. I discuss the extent to which young women can only ever have access to these ideals in gendered ways in Chapter 4. This is an issue I also explore in greater detail in subsequent chapters, as I look at the problems and possibilities opened up for young women in Australia in the 1950s and early 1960s as they encountered modern ideals of individuality and personhood in quite different forms in a range of institutional or social settings.

3 / Growing up as a modern individual: on youth and modernity in the 1950s

The term 'modern' had a wide currency in the 1950s. Projects of modernization proliferated and were celebrated in terms of their modernity. In Australia, a diverse range of undertakings were discussed in these terms: the building of dams, highways, nuclear power research stations, city skyscrapers and programmes of slum clearance. Homes were to be modern, as were the families that lived within them; educational institutions were modern and young people were to be prepared for their place in 'the modern world' by remaining in them for an extended period of time. So, too, were places of work to be modern, and the jobs advertised as available in them were said to be attractive because of their modernity.

Alongside this rhetoric, many academic investigations appeared, concerned to examine what was referred to as 'the modern condition'. These were particularly popular in the USA but they had their counterparts elsewhere. Many of these diagnoses of the modern world shared an apparent preoccupation with youth, with the problems, as they saw it, of young people being able to grow up properly under circumstances which Paul Goodman labelled 'absurd'. Yet a number of recent studies have suggested that this identification of youth as both symbol and victim of modernity is a phenomenon not only of this period, but is characteristic of the way in which particular anxieties about modernity as a set of social conditions have typically been expressed since the eighteenth century.

In this chapter, I outline this latter argument, particularly as it has been elaborated in a study by Franco Moretti of the *Bildungsroman* as a cultural form. His analysis is drawn on throughout this book. I then move to a discussion of the specific way in which modernity was conceptualized in a number of key texts published in the 1950s and early 1960s, examining how they positioned young people as symbols and victims of 'the modern'. I am interested in how a body of literature emerges in the 1950s that translates the dilemmas of the eighteenth-century *Bildungsroman*, as described by Moretti, into a set of normative prescriptions about youth. Studies specifically about the position of young people in 'modern Australia' will be analysed in the following chapter.

Youth as symbol of modernity

Franco Moretti, in his book *The Way of the World* (1987), argues that the image of youth 'acts as a sort of symbolic concentrate of the uncertainties and tensions of an entire cultural system'.[1] The more a society perceives itself as unstable and precarious in its legitimation of the social order or the social norms of its culture, the stronger is the image of youth and its use to register these anxieties. In stable communities, the question of how new generations are to be integrated into the social order does not arise. Such is the case, says Moretti, in those societies which we now designate 'traditional', that is, in societies where who one is is a matter of birth; identity derives from the status and roles ascribed to each individual – by the family they are born into, and their position in that family. The modern world, on the other hand, characterized by the breakdown of such social relations, makes growing up far more problematic. This period in a person's life is no longer prescribed, no longer a predictable time of apprenticeship.

At the turn of the eighteenth century, Europe was plunged into modernity. In the attempt to make that experience meaningful and to deal with the tensions which arose in this context, the figure of youth achieved, Moretti argues, symbolic centrality. Youth was conceptualized as a group with the attributes of restless energy, a desire for mobility and experimentation and holding great expectations about the future. Moretti identifies the *Bildungsroman* – the novel of formation or education – as one cultural form which set out to explore this use of the figure of youth as a way of articulating and solving the quandaries facing modern societies. The central dilemma of modern bourgeois civilization, as it emerged in eighteenth-century Europe, according to Moretti, was 'the conflict between the ideal of *self-determination* and the equally imperious demands of *socialization*'.[2] The ideal of the self-determining or self-legislating individual meant that social order could no longer be maintained by the force of tradition, and consent to that order could not be gained through the exercise of the authority of a sovereign form of power. The perpetuation of the current system of social relations had to be

secured through other means. The problem was posed in terms of
how the 'free individual' could be required to be, at the same time,
the 'convinced citizen' – not as a fearful subject, but as one who
perceives 'the social norms as *one's own*'.[3]

The figure of youth in the *Bildungsroman* provided an apparently
harmonious solution to this dilemma. Such novels tell the story of
youth as a period in which the modern individual enjoys the freedom
to make him/her self, to determine what his or her identity will be.
Youth is the time of adventure, experimentation, journeys and
growth. These novels characteristically conclude with marriage,
symbolizing, Moretti suggests, the end of the journey and of the
period of becoming. This social pact between two individuals – 'freely
chosen' – is an allegory for the social contract between the individual
and the social world. The renunciation of the freedom and the risks
involved in endlessly seeking to make one's self, to direct one's own
life, is associated with maturity in the *Bildungsroman*. The meaning
of the events of youth, according to this cultural form, lies only in
its leading to a particularly marked ending.[4] The modern notion that
youth as an experience is circumscribed by the necessities of the
biological process of growing up lends weight to the implication
that modernity, too, is under control, an experience which can
be limited and made human. In the classical *Bildungsroman*, the
modern individual, on reaching maturity, exchanges 'the "sweet and
intimate" feeling of belonging to a system that literally "takes care
of everything", as opposed to the possibility of directing one's own
life "to one's own risk and danger"'.[5]

The *Bildungsroman*, says Moretti, represents youth as concerned
only with mobility and a restless, dissatisfied exploration of the
social spaces available to them. It does so in order to make meaningful precisely these aspects of the experience of modernity.
The choice of 'youth' as the 'specific material sign' of this new
epoch serves to define modernity's essence as 'a world that seeks
its meaning in the future rather than the past'.[6] But in these novels
a sense of closure is retained; the world of novels like Goethe's
Wilhelm Meister is not truly 'open', an authority still exists which
can decree the end of the period of youth, of the period in which
individuals can be preoccupied with the constant making of their
personalities.

By the middle of the nineteenth century, the boundless energy of
bourgeois capitalism with its promises of the endless opportunities
for individuals to transform their lives simply through the purchasing
of goods – through having – undermined all such notions of closure.
It now seemed possible for the individual to seek constantly to 'put
aside one's being and forge a new one';[7] such activity becomes an

end in itself and youth, it appears, need no longer be anything but itself. The attempt made by the *Bildungsroman* to suggest that the period of becoming, which it associated with youth, will necessarily come to an end in the lives of modern individuals with their attainment of maturity, could no longer be sustained without considerable strain in the context of the changes now being wrought in the social and cultural order.

The modernist tradition of cultural critique, examined in the previous chapter, emerged in the context of these changes. This critique claimed that processes of cultural modernization stimulate and enlarge the individual's consciousness to such an extent that it becomes impossible to know one's own self. The apparently limitless opportunities to be something else, and to be a multiplicity of things, undermines the individual's capacity to form the self into a coherent unity, to determine that self as having a specific form. While the figure of woman in such contexts registers concerns about the extent to which cultural modernization simply makes people its objects rather than subjects capable of determining their own lives,[8] the figure of youth continued to be employed more specifically to articulate anxieties that modernization will undermine the forces of cultural and political authority. The consumer culture of modern capitalism threatens to create a new generation of young people, it is claimed, with a narcissistic desire to last forever and to remain apart from and with no responsibilities to the community as a whole. Such were the claims of a number of significant texts of cultural critique which appeared in the 1950s.

Youth and the post-war era

In the wake of the Second World War, the place held by youth in discussions of the 'modern condition' in different Western countries varied according to the sorts of transformations occurring in their social, political and cultural structures. John Clarke and his co-authors argue that one of the most striking and visible manifestations of social change in post-war Britain was the way in which 'youth' appeared as an emergent category at this time. This term signified a social problem, something that needed investigation, monitoring and official intervention, but it served, too, these authors comment, as a 'cornerstone in the construction of understandings, interpretations and quasi-explanations *about* the period'.[9] In Britain, the discussion of youth at that time registered both hopes and anxieties about the nature of social and cultural change and, in particular, about the breaking up of traditional class cultures.

A key text in these terms was Richard Hoggart's *The Uses of Literacy* (1957). This book played a pioneering role in the development of cultural studies as a field of investigation and as a critical project. Using his literary training in practical criticism, Hoggart set out to 'read' the working-class culture he had encountered as a child and to record its sensibilities, its structure of feeling. The critical point of this endeavour was to demonstrate what he saw as the impoverishing effect of the new technologies of cultural production on this culture. According to Hoggart, mass culture destroyed the ability working-class people had possessed in the past to exert some form of control over their own lives. It undermined the strengths and capacities they had built up over a period of time through the collective processes of developing a working-class culture.

In this analysis, Hoggart conjured up images of alienated youths lounging in milk-bars, listening to the juke box, in order to represent all that he found most disturbing about the cultural transformations he sought to identify and understand. He depicted young people as victims of the false promises and the glittering but empty pleasures offered by the new cultural industries. In this account of social and cultural change in post-war Britain, the category of youth registered Hoggart's anxieties about modernization in the field of cultural production in particular. Hoggart claimed that they were vulnerable to the forces of modernization, to being manipulated and hence made merely objects of the changes it brought to the social and political order, not simply because of their age, but because they had been cut off from traditional cultural resources.[10]

In Britain in the 1950s, then, youth served as a focus for anxieties about what Stuart Hall has referred to as 'the cultural impact of the long-delayed entry' of that country 'into the modern world'.[11] New forms of affluence, the consumer society and changes such as the development of a mass secondary school system challenged the hierarchical structure of that society. Though its economic structures had been modernized in the previous two centuries, its social and cultural order had remained largely untouched. As Moretti notes, in the eighteenth and nineteenth centuries, it was not a society which could or even wanted to identify with youth as a figure concerned with adventure and social mobility.[12] Its value system had remained stable through the successful merging of tradition and progress; the Second World War brought about the rapid dismantling of that stability.

Across the Atlantic, youth also became the focus of analyses of the modern condition in the 1950s. Indeed, in the USA, studies and writings about youth became a major industry after the Second

World War. In this instance, however, youth served as a symbol for exploring a continuing ambivalence about modernization and democracy, rather than as a means of registering and talking about their arrival. Two books, in particular, illustrate vividly the way youth was constituted as a symbol for this ambivalence in the USA in the first decade or so after the war: David Riesman's *The Lonely Crowd* (1950) and Paul Goodman's *Growing Up Absurd* (1961). In addition, these texts played a key role in establishing youth or adolescent studies as an increasingly legitimate field of investigation in the 1950s and 1960s not just in the USA but also in other countries, such as Australia.

Riesman's diagnosis of modernity is probably best known for his claim that modern society produces two main character types – the 'inner-directed' and the 'other-directed'. His book can be read on at least two levels. As a document of a particular historical moment, it can be examined for what it tells us about the changing nature of subjectivity in post-Second World War America. At another level, it can be seen as contributing to traditions of modernist cultural critique, broadly defined, which have typically constituted the feminine and the figure of 'youth' in specific ways. Riesman argued that the 'other-directed' character was becoming increasingly dominant in modern, metropolitan America. He identified modern patterns of child-rearing, progressive notions of education, the pressures of the peer group, and the mass media as the major forces producing this change. This personality type could be characterized, he claimed, by the way in which 'their contemporaries are the source of direction for the individual – either those known to him or those with whom he is indirectly acquainted, through friends and through the mass media.'[13] Other-direction involves a redefinition of the self away from external achievements towards interactional or inner qualities: the 'other-directed person wants to be loved rather than esteemed'.[14] Similarly, the system of social rewards and social advancement in modern America, Riesman declared, emphasized personality rather than achievement. The canons of success in this society had shifted to an emphasis on gaining the approval of others by a presentation of one's self as 'in tune' with them.[15] Young people, he claimed, were particularly susceptible to this culture. The loss of inner confidence among adults in the face of the massive changes occurring in the technological orientation of society, as well as in its system of values, left youth vulnerable and confused.[16]

The inner-directed character type, according to Riesman, emerged in the Renaissance period of European history, but had subsequently been taken up by different communities to a greater or lesser extent until recent times. Inner-directed persons believe that their characters are to be worked on throughout their lives. Theirs is a 'scrutinizing self', monitoring and judging itself in this constant process of self-making.[17] The source of the criteria used by this scrutinizing self is the training received from parents or elders early in life. A 'psychological gyroscope', Riesman claimed, is set in place by socialization processes and by the clear directions given about life goals in one's early years by these figures of authority.

Riesman claimed to be documenting changes occurring in the dominant personality structures in the USA. These were produced by the transformation of the economic and social basis of society – in particular, by changes in the level of economic activity and population growth. Riesman's method of describing the transformation occurring in the processes of identity formation by defining a number of character-types limited his analysis of those changes. Nevertheless, his account did point to some significant shifts and his attempt to identify the historically changing nature of subjectivity – of how we understand who we are and how we can and should operate in the world – did demonstrate the importance of the post-war era in significantly reshaping forms of personal identification. His focus on child-rearing practices, changes in the orientation and organization of schooling, the mass media and the new types of persons required by the bureaucratic organization of work, indicated key processes involved in bringing about such changes.

Riesman thus declared himself primarily engaged in a descriptive sociological study rather than a prescriptive project. In additional prefaces to new editions of this book, he insisted that he had not viewed the 'other-directed' character type as more conformist than the 'inner-directed'. He claimed that each character formation produced conformity. The early socialization of the inner-directed person ensured acquiescence to the social norms of the society; the constant need for social approval of the other-directed person achieved the same effect but through rather different means. In his concluding chapter, however, Riesman did also attempt to outline the character structure he believed desirable to meet the challenges of post-war society. He designated this personality type the 'autonomous person'. Such an individual, he proposed, must have, at one and the same time, a clear vision for the future, and a pragmatic concern for everyday life in which the needs of others and oneself are not sacrificed for the sake of the relentless pursuit of one's ideals.[18]

In her discussion of social science texts of the 1950s, Wini Breines argues that authors like Riesman were documenting changes underway in American manhood rather than a more general transformation in personality structures. She looks for a gender subtext in these analyses and the extent to which, in her terms, they articulated fears about emasculation. 'In hindsight', she says, 'it becomes clear that the skills and traits of the other-directed personality are more traditionally feminine than masculine.'[19] As a description of changes in the type of person required by the new bureaucratic structures of the period, she suggests, Riesman's analysis expressed a powerful anxiety that these would constitute an attack on manhood itself. Breines' critique of Riesman draws attention to how the dichotomy he constituted between two ways of being in the world relied upon an implicit set of understandings and valuations of constructions of the masculine and of the feminine in Western culture.

While this reading of Riesman provides some useful suggestions about the nature of his preoccupations, his work also needs to be examined for insights into the significant transformations in the subjectivities of both young men and women which were occurring in the post-war era. Those changes may have had different implications for men and women to the extent that new dominant vocabularies about the self may have sat more or less easily with other gendered forms of identification also in circulation at this time. But we need to look at these latter forms of subjectivity as changing too. Breines suggests that the traits of the other-directed person are traditionally feminine rather than masculine. Such a claim tends to obscure the extent to which dominant forms of masculinity and femininity were also being reworked in significant ways at this time.[20] Riesman's characterization of the other-directed personality as involved in a constant search for the approval of others and a presentation of one's self as 'in tune with others' as a description of a particular way of operating in the world implies a degree of 'impression management'[21] new, I suggest, for both men and women at this time.

By the same token, Riesman can be used to provide insights into the way in which patterns of growing up were being massively transformed in this period. His intimations of the changing role of the education system, and of the increased importance of the mass media and shifts in the workings of contemporary family units, do indicate important sites for such an analysis. However, his argument in this instance is also significant at another level. As I have already indicated, in constituting youth as a group particularly vulnerable to the changes occurring, Riesman contributed to a tradition of registering certain anxieties about modernity through the symbolic figure of youth. Yet, precisely in writing about and investigating youth as a group 'at risk', he also contributed to an increasing preoccupation among certain professional agencies and modern institutions with intervening in and monitoring the lives of young people.

Diagnoses of the 'modern' by authors like Riesman in the post-war era contributed to the definition of this age category as a separate social group, designating them, in the process, as 'a social problem', something which society needed to supervise and regulate in specific ways. This point will be discussed further in the final section of this chapter.

Paul Goodman's book, *Growing Up Absurd* (1961), can also be read as functioning on these various levels. It, too, was a diagnosis of modernity which used the figure of youth to articulate concerns about what he referred to as 'the organized system'. Modern times, he argued, have been formed by the accumulation of a series of missed revolutions. The promises of modern technological change, of urban development, of democratization, of the growth of modern science, of the extension of education, had not been fulfilled. Instead, modern America, he claimed, was a closed society in which the rat race dominated and no worthwhile goals existed for young people to pursue in the course of their growing up. Indeed, it was, he affirmed, a society which made it impossible to grow up.

Goodman insisted that it was not youth who were to blame for their failure to grow up. He counterposed his analysis to popular rhetoric of the 1950s which complained of poor socialization practices in modern society or the lack of a sense of belonging provided by the contemporary culture. The problem, he argued, had nothing to do with such empty claims. It was an issue of the failure of modern America to be sufficiently modern – to grasp the revolutionary character of modernity in which traditions are constantly shattered and change occurs with an unending speed. Instead of embracing these characteristics of the modern world, 'the organized system' sought to close off or control this restless spirit and the opportunities it offered to create a new type of community, a new world.

Goodman was quite explicit about the issue of gender in his analysis. As far as he was concerned, the tasks of the modern individual – those that should be undertaken by the young person in the process of growing up – need not concern young women. They did not need to 'make something' of themselves. Their worthwhile futures, he asserted, were already made, guaranteed by their biologies. Women did not need to worry about being useful; their child-bearing capacity guaranteed their usefulness. The existence of a closed society only became an issue for young women, Goodman commented, in that it made it difficult for boys to grow to be men: 'If the husband is running the rat race of the organized system, there is not much father for the children.'[22] Goodman's text clearly can be interpreted in the terms suggested by Breines about the

preoccupation of 1950s social science texts with the changes occurring in American manhood. According to Goodman, young women
were not subject to the contingencies of the modern world and
hence burdened by freedom, by the responsibility of 'making' themselves. And, again, it is significant that Berman, who refers to
Goodman as writing within the modernist tradition, does not comment on this construction of woman as somehow outside or as the
'Other' of modernity. In Goodman's analysis, the tasks of the modern
individual are those that define a virile and independent manhood.

Youth as a separate category of person

Both Riesman's and Goodman's texts need to be seen in the context
of a society emerging from the traumas of the Second World War
and of a political climate which constituted the contemporary world
as still being very much 'at war'. Democracy, it was claimed, was
under constant threat from communism – the enemy within as well
as without. In this context, both authors sought to juggle the requirements seen as central to a liberal democracy of the creation of
a society in which individuals embrace the culture of freedom to
become self-determining, autonomous beings. Such a social order
distinguished the USA from the contemporary 'Other' of communism. At the same time, Riesman and Goodman were conscious of
the demands of social integration, of the need to find a mechanism
to bind individuals – 'freely' – to the social order as modern citizens.
Youth, in the writings of these authors, was a symbolic figure for the
excitement, promise and dangers of modern Western civilization.
    Yet, in focusing on youth, these writers contributed to the con-
struction of youth as a separate category of person. Declaring young
people particularly susceptible to contemporary pressures of conformity, they defined them as a social group 'at risk', in need of
monitoring and social programmes of assistance. At the same time,
in claiming the need to produce a population of self-legislating
individuals, Riesman and Goodman provided arguments for the
necessity of augmenting and extending the period of youth. All
young people, in these terms, were described as 'youth' with particular needs and with shared concerns: these characteristics required
that they remain 'youth' for a definite and extended period of time
to ensure their successful negotiation of the tasks of growing up, the
tasks of becoming a modern individual.
    Though Riesman and Goodman were as much concerned with
modernity as with youth, their studies heralded and contributed to
a burgeoning area in the human sciences in the 1950s: adolescent

studies. Primarily either psychological or sociological in orientation, these studies set out to investigate and monitor 'the adolescent experience', as well as to specify what that experience should involve.[23] This field of investigation would increasingly in the 1950s translate the notion of the tasks of becoming a modern individual, as I will show in the following chapter, into a set of normalizing discourses concerned to describe in detail how these tasks must be undertaken for the young person to grow up 'properly'. As a period in a person's life associated in contemporary Western culture with experimentation and self-definition, youth now became the focus of a body of knowledge and techniques of social intervention which set out to ensure that it took on precisely that form. In particular, the science of developmental psychology, which became increasingly professionalized in the 1950s, would seek to monitor the lives of all young people and to assist them in undertaking the tasks, as it understood and interpreted them, of the modern individual.

Yet, Riesman's and Goodman's work can be distinguished from this field of human science not simply by the focus on modernity. They engaged with the dilemma seen to lie at the heart of this experience; namely, the contradictions which Moretti describes as central for the modern Western mentality – the contradictions between the desire for freedom and the desire for happiness or belonging, between the dynamism and restlessness of contingency and the need to make meaningful, and human, the experience of this world of constant change.[24] This was the dilemma the *Bildungsroman* sought to resolve through compromise in depicting the tasks of the modern individual as ending when youth is relinquished for maturity. The individual in this narrative 'freely chooses' happiness, belonging, an end to the story of 'becoming', making a self – characteristically symbolized by marriage – just as the modern citizen 'chooses' social integration. The contradictions were acknowledged at the same time as a resolution was sought in this cultural form. Similarly, Riesman and Goodman confronted this dilemma as they attempted to interpret the cultural ideal of the autonomous, self-defining individual and the problems posed to its realization in the contemporary social order.

Adolescent studies, however, frequently sought to eliminate the contradiction. As I will show in the following chapter in greater detail, developmental psychology, for instance, claimed that the natural processes of biology determined the period of youth and its time of a proper ending. It declared growing up involved a steady process of throwing off the 'need' or 'urge' felt by young people to seek autonomy, independence, self-actualization. Though they found the meaning of youth lay in its proper ending, as did the

Bildungsroman, psychologically-based, adolescent studies saw no need for compromise. Nature organized youth and maturity as simply stages in human development. The role of the human sciences was to assist in organizing the lives of young people to enable them to go through these stages at appropriate moments in their lives. Incorrect or undesirable social conditions could distort or bloat 'the needs of the adolescent'; surveillance and intervention in the lives of young people was required to bring the processes of growing up to a satisfactory point of closure.

In the following two chapters, I look at how these normative prescriptions of adolescent studies emerge primarily in the context of the democratization of secondary school. My argument here is simply that texts like those by Riesman and Goodman contributed to and provided legitimacy for the practices and claims of adolescent psychology as an emerging field in the human sciences. Though their preoccupations focused on modernity rather than youth and their arguments eschewed normalizing prescriptions about the necessary closure of the period of youth, their writings appeared as part of a more general call for the need to monitor and intervene in the lives of young people and to require all of this group to be 'youth' for a specific period in their lives. Yet, while Riesman and Goodman recognized the notion of the self-determining, autonomous individual as a cultural ideal or historical project with no necessary point of closure, adolescent psychology translated this ideal into a requirement of nature and found both its meaning and ending to be dictated by the 'needs' of biology.

In defining the tasks of the modern individual, however, neither Riesman nor Goodman acknowledged the way in which the sociological conditions they criticized did not necessarily ensure that this form of personhood was automatically accessible to or considered appropriate for all members of the population. Their critique of modernization had focused on how social forces undermined or distorted the way in which those tasks were understood; but they were not concerned to challenge the extent to which material conditions, as well as the circulation of other vocabularies about how certain social groups should understand themselves and their place in the world, constituted that form of personhood as more appropriate or indeed perhaps only possible for certain types of people. As I have indicated, Goodman simply asserted that young women need not bother with the requirements for modern individuals to make themselves. In their world, he declared, contingency did not exist; their roles and their futures were predetermined by their biology.

Only young men, it seemed, had to take on the burden and the risks of defining themselves, the pleasures and the responsibility of becoming self-legislating. Riesman, on the other hand, did suggest that young women increasingly could not rely on taking on the roles they had observed as organizing the lives of their mothers and their grandmothers. They, too, could no longer rely on tradition; they did, according to Riesman, have to face the contingent nature of the modern world and make a self and a world for themselves. But he did not contemplate the way in which his specifications about how those tasks should be undertaken might not fit comfortably with the material conditions in which young women found themselves, nor with the continuing social expectation that their lives would be organized in different ways to those of young men.

In their description of the characteristics required of the modern individual, Riesman and Goodman decried certain ways of being in the world and positively valued others. Wini Breines has argued that these differentiations entailed an affirmation of the traditionally masculine and a negation of the feminine. I want to propose a slightly different interpretation of their work by suggesting that their analyses registered the processes through which the subjectivities of both young men and young women were being transformed in fundamental ways in this period. The supposed character of the feminine was as much in flux as were notions of the masculine. At the same time, they were pointing to and participating in the massive changes occurring in the way in which modern Western societies organized and understood the processes of growing up for young people. Their work may have been driven by anxieties about how these changes were undermining the extent to which the cultural ideal of the modern individual continued to shape societal expectations about what the growing up of young men involved; but it may also point towards the possibility that the relationship between the feminine and modern was being reworked in fundamental ways as well in this period.

The following chapters take up this issue in a specific historical context. I look at how the cultural ideal of the modern personality as a self-determining identity was translated into concrete terms in a range of settings in Australia in the 1950s and early 1960s. I consider the contradictory aspects of the way this ideal became a set of tasks for young people to undertake for a limited period in their lives, as well as the particular forms in which young women encountered these tasks. I am concerned with the possibilities and difficulties created for young women in the transformation of the organization and definition of growing up and girlhood in Australia at this time.

4 / Growing up in modern Australia: the study of young people in Australia in the 1950s

Notions of the 'modern' were recruited in a variety of contexts in Australia in the post-war era. The term served two main purposes in its usage in popular texts such as daily newspapers and women's magazines. First, it insisted on a difference between this historical moment and what had gone before – it served to create a sense of closure on the previous periods of uncertainty, on the economic hardship of the depression years and the social and political turmoil caused by war. Second, it claimed that the democratization of desire,[1] which had begun earlier in the century but had been interrupted by these upheavals, would not only be resumed, but would now be transformed into a democratization of life worlds. Mass-produced consumer goods had become increasingly available in the first half of the twentieth century. New retailing techniques, and in particular the establishment of department stores, had made these goods not accessible to all, yet visible to all – available to their gaze. In the 1920s, the use of advertising strategies further enhanced the sense that everyone could soon have the opportunity to enjoy the same material pleasures and comforts. The celebration of the 'modern' after the Second World War contained the promise that these desires could now be realized. This term was used to invoke a sense of progress and prosperity and of the capacity of the free enterprise system to create a world in which all had access, not simply to the same dreams, but to the opportunity to make those dreams reality in their everyday lives.

This chapter begins with a consideration of how both popular representations and contemporary social commentators in Australia in the 1950s and 1960s invoked gendered images of 'the modern'. This material provides the setting for a discussion of key Australian studies of young people in this period and, in particular, of one major investigation, the report by W.F. Connell and colleagues at the University of Sydney, *Growing Up in an Australian City* (1959). This book both relied upon and enhanced the legitimacy of developmental psychology as a tool of teacher training in Australia. I consider the growth of this human science and the ideas of the American psychologist, R.J. Havighurst, whose work was immensely influential in this context. Finally, I turn to discuss the extent to which the norms articulated in such texts are implicitly gendered. The point of this discussion is, as I have indicated in previous chapters, to begin to discuss the range of ways in which young women in this period encountered the cultural ideal of the self-determining individual, not in a disembedded abstract way, but as a set of tasks with particular limits and particular meanings.

Australia – 'the lusty youth'[2]

Popular representations of Australia in the 1950s as 'a lusty youth' or 'adolescent' in the modern world conjured up a sense that it was just about to join that world, with all the spirit and energy supposedly characteristic of youth. As the Melbourne-based newspaper, the *Age*, declared at the beginning of 1951: 'For Australia, this next half century is one of unlimited promise – promise of development, of growth into economic adulthood.'[3] And, indeed, the range of modernization projects undertaken in the 1950s appeared to indicate that this was precisely what was happening. The building of highways, dams, new automated factories, the Holden car project, atomic bomb testing sites, shopping centres, skyscrapers and new schools were all welcomed in these terms. Expectations about the capacity of postwar Australia to create a democracy of life worlds had been firmly encouraged during the war by the formation of the Department of Postwar Reconstruction in 1942 under the direction of the Curtin Labor Government. This Department set up various mechanisms of social engineering (such as the Commonwealth Housing Commission), at the same time as it affirmed the capacity of a vigorous free enterprise system to provide full employment. Projects of modernization begun in the years after the war appeared to promise that these expectations would be realized.

In representations of modernization projects like dams and power stations, the 'modern' was about adventure, mastery, the dominance of nature by man, excitement and the nation's prosperity and progress. Press reports, for instance, of the building of the Snowy Mountains Hydro-Electric Scheme, drew on and reworked these key themes of modernity. Initiated by the Federal Labor Government in

1949 and taking 25 years to complete, this Scheme involved the building of many power stations, dams and tunnels and the moving of whole towns to new sites: a project of truly Faustian proportions. Newspaper articles described it as 'our greatest and most courageous Australian effort to bend nature to man's minds for the benefits of generations to come'; a 'colossal game with nature'. Drilling machines and bulldozers 'changing the course of waterfalls' became a 'new romance'; and '[t]he men who are constructing the Snowy Mountains project' were acclaimed as 'men of the outdoors, engineers dedicated to grand concepts and achievements, men with an affection for delicate instruments or mammoth machines'.[4] In these descriptions of the trail-blazing, austere greatness of projects of modernization, modernity was clearly linked to masculinity. Men and machines were to tame nature, to bend it to 'man's' needs, to 'master' and control the universe.

In other settings, however, modernity served the everyday feminine. In this instance, modernization appeared to be devoted to the project of the democratization of life worlds in which all would have access to the comforts and benefits of modern living. This was the promise and the dream recruited by the consumer industries and their advertising agencies to persuade women to identify themselves as consumers. An advertisement by a Sydney department store, Hordern Bros, clearly articulated the sense of excitement and plenty increasingly employed by these industries in the 1950s:

> This is the day of the individualist! This is the day of self expression in all things, exciting days because we are daring to be interesting. Our clothes show more imagination in cut, colour and texture. We are living better, more happily, more enjoyably. Entertaining is more gracious, more amusing. More people are travelling everywhere . . . Hordern Bros., a store of very special individuality, sophistication and excitement, invites you to spend a day browsing through the exqisitely [sic] re-decorated floors – each the most advanced in modern decor yet seen in Sydney.[5]

Such publicity statements were directed at augmenting popular needs and desires, but at the same time they promoted an image of women's access to the benefits of the modern, albeit in a very particular form. This issue will be explored further in Chapter 7.[6]

The reality of living in Australia for many women in the 1950s was, of course, very different. Certainly, the consumer industries achieved an ever-increasing democratization of desire. The wish to own your own home, to buy a car, to have all the latest household appliances, to buy new clothes for yourself and your children, to own a radio and, after 1956, a television, no doubt was shared by a large section of the population. The post-war economic boom and the associated high levels of employment, the increasing levels of employment among married women,[7] the greater use of bank mortgages to buy houses[8] and the burgeoning of hire purchase credit schemes to buy many of the household commodities, all contributed to an appearance that these dreams were now being realized for all Australians. Indeed, by the early 1960s, a widespread belief existed, according to Greg Whitwell, that universal affluence had been achieved and poverty abolished. It was not until Ronald Henderson and his associates at the University of Melbourne began to publish their work on poverty in Australia in the middle of that decade that such beliefs were seriously challenged.[9] Nor was it publicly acknowledged, until government policy on both immigration and the Australian Aboriginal population began to change from assimilation to multiculturalism, that the realities and the dreams of large numbers of people living in Australia were very different to those symbolized by the domestic idyll of suburbia and consumerism as uniting all ordinary Australians.

A number of voices critical of this particular dream of the modern began to be heard by the late 1950s. These critics did not, however, attack the gap between the dream and the reality of people's lives; they challenged the character of the dream itself. Russel Ward's *The Australian Legend* (1958) and A.A. Phillips's *The Australian Tradition* (1958) celebrated the man of the land, the man of 'open spaces', as the authentic Australian. George Johnston, in his novel *My Brother Jack*, published a few years later in 1964, depicted his main character, Jack Meredith, as borne down, emasculated by the petty mundanity of suburban life. These critics did not reject modernity as such. They applauded the heroic image of a conquering, pioneering, austere masculinity – the modern individual in a particular guise – but scorned the world of domesticity and everyday life of modern suburbia as not a fit place for men. Although different in many ways, these authors shared with the American 1950s critics of the modern, a similar concern with the increasing public presence of a particular femininity and the consequences of these changes for men.

Apparently taking a quite different approach, Donald Horne, in *The Lucky Country* (1964), embraced the suburbanization of Australia and a new masculinity that could feel at home in that world. This domesticated Australian male had become 'the dinkum Aussie', whose informality, egalitarian spirit and very ordinariness made him truly Australian. Australia, according to Horne, was a country where all could have their heart's desire: a house, a car, oysters, suntans, cans of asparagus, lobsters, seaside holidays, golf, tennis, surfing, fishing, gardening. It was 'the lucky country' where the 'image of Australia is of a man in an open-necked shirt solemnly enjoying an icecream. His kiddy beside him.'[10]

Reasserting the centrality of masculinity in this modern world of suburban Australia, Horne went on to warn of the dangers that could arise from complacency. His reference to 'the lucky country' was intended to be ironic.[11] The ready embrace of modern consumer society by Australians, he claimed, indicated their strengths – their flexibility and their egalitarianism; it could, however, also be their downfall. Their general contentment with things as they are, said Horne, made no demands on their leaders. The Australian population was being let down by politicians and businessmen alike; these figures lacked drive and, most importantly, creativity. Horne's call was for a more educated population, a more imaginative leadership and an embracing of the opportunities of modern capitalism. In this analysis, Australia was not in the process of becoming a modern society; it was no mere adolescent in these terms. Indeed, part of Horne's purpose was to argue that Australia was very much part of the modern world, but risked being returned to a relationship of dependency, of becoming economically, once again, a colonial society.

In more recent work, Horne deplores the emphasis on youth which he sees as emerging in the late 1960s in Australia. He criticizes both the hedonism encouraged by the booming teenage market and what he sees as the 'simple optimism' of university radicals of this period.[12] Yet, contemporary interpretations of his book of the 1960s discuss its social impact in terms of the shoring up of optimism and its role in encouraging young people in Australia to believe that the future belonged to them.[13] His emphasis on education and on the need for a new form of leadership suggested that it was precisely the new generation of young people who could ensure that Australia maintained and secured its place in the modern world. In his diagnosis of contemporary Australia, youth were not the victims of modernity, they were its symbols and possible saviours.

The relationship between the modern and the feminine was, then, a contested one. The consumer economy, gaining strength in Australia in the 1950s, encouraged women to become involved in modernity not, as Martin Pumphrey notes in a different context, in an abstract theoretical form, but through concrete ideas of fashion and lifestyle.[14] Images of suburban life served by modern inventions and the continual excitement and sense of pleasures to be had in the world of fashion spoke of a humanized version of modernity whose project was to democratize and make everyday life a sphere of comfort and pleasure. While Donald Horne set out to reassert the centrality of the masculine figure to this modern environment of the everyday, the celebrations of the capacity of modernization projects to transform and dominate the social and natural environment challenged this version of modernity. Discussions and reports on Australian youth in the 1950s and early 1960s both drew on and contributed to these debates about the promises and dangers of modernity for this 'youthful nation'.

Investigating Australian youth

The contingency of modern social arrangements, the rapid character of technological change, and the uncertainty of the future in the context of a world attempting to deal with the massive and catastrophic character of modern warfare, were all identified as phenomena which made the young particularly vulnerable. Similarly, the uncertainty of Australia's place in a world of rapid change and modernization was thought to create difficulties for young people to understand what was required of them in the process of their growing up. Like their overseas counterparts, Australian youth were both symbol and victim of modernity in the studies of adolescents conducted in the 1950s.

These investigations declared that a set of dilemmas faced Australian youth clearly akin to those organizing the narrative of the classic *Bildungsroman*. Young people, various reports and academic texts claimed, had to become both responsible citizens at the same time as they learnt to take advantage of the freedom and autonomy made possible by the contingency of modern social arrangements. They were both responsible to and for democracy. The *Bildungsroman* narrative, as we have seen in the previous chapter, sought to resolve these apparently competing claims of freedom and socialization: the needs of the individual and the needs of society. In the Australian literature of the 1950s about youth, the notion of 'the adjustment of youth' became a central theme similarly attempting to balance what were represented as the two sets of requirements of a modern democratic social order. In a world that had been torn apart, it was argued, by the struggle between individualism and extreme totalitarianism – by those who placed supreme value on the individual and those who found it in the state – youth became both the hope for, and those most at risk, in the attempt to create a different world.[15]

A report published by the Australian Council for Educational

Research (ACER) in 1951, *The Adjustment of Youth*, framed its considerations principally in terms of these preoccupations. The central problem facing young people in the process of growing up in the modern world, the authors declared, was 'to realize to the utmost their potentialities for physical, mental and moral development while preparing themselves to fill worthy places as adult members of society'.[16] This problem, they claimed, was a problem of 'social adjustment' in which the 'maturing powers of the individual' have to be balanced against the demands and influences of the 'social environment'; the 'needs of the individual' against the 'needs of society'.[17] According to the authors of this report, ensuring that these two sets of claims became complementary, made the project of the 'adjustment of youth', then, not just a personal one for each individual to make in the process of their growing up, but one of great political significance for the whole of society. Yet the problems facing young people in this post-war period had multiplied, they maintained, precisely because the world had become so divided by political and social differences. It was an increasingly complex world to which young people must adjust themselves in the process of their growing up. The role of the education professionals and the associated fields of knowledge and expertise such as medicine, psychology, genetics and sociology, it was argued, had become vital in making sure that the needs of individuals and society could be made to complement each other in assisting the young in the process of their growing up.[18]

And it was precisely in these terms that this literature claimed that the dilemma, which the *Bildungsroman* had posed as fundamental to modernity, could be readily solved. The expansion of the work and influence of the human sciences would resolve any tensions which were understood to exist between the needs of the individual and the needs of society. Experts in these fields could be relied on to determine what were reasonable claims to be made in the name of these two sets of needs. And the expansion and modernizing of post-primary or secondary education would enable their expertise to be put to work.[19] The proper organization of the process of growing up would ensure that all would undergo a period of becoming, a period of self-making, but it would also ensure that this 'need' for self-definition and autonomy would come to a satisfactory point of closure. While the *Bildungsroman* had relied on a belief, and hope, that the individual would inevitably always reach maturity, this Australian adolescent studies literature, like the overseas material, argued for the increased intervention of appropriate groups of professionals to ensure that young people attained maturity in an appropriate manner.

W.F. Connell and his colleagues in their study of Sydney's youth adopted a similar stance to the ACER report. It announced itself an investigation produced in the context of training teachers, and it subsequently became a key text used in teacher training, particularly in New South Wales. But in the framing statements at the beginning and end of this study, it claimed to be much more than a simple report of what young people were thinking and doing in the early 1950s in one city in Australia. It set out to make programmatic statements about the needs of young people and the needs of Australian society. The particular problem facing young people in Australia, according to Connell *et al.*, was the lack of a coherent Australian identity. Australia and its cities had now clearly entered the modern world and a distinct urban culture had emerged, they claimed; yet its standards and values remained 'misty and unclear', 'indistinct, unformulated and subject to change'.[20] Faced with such uncertainty and surrounded by a rapidly growing number of social agencies which sought to tell them how to lead their lives, how were young people to choose?

The study surveyed 100 000 Sydney adolescents – approximately 10 per cent of young people, the researchers calculated, who were between the ages of 13 and 18 in that city. In addition, they drew on interviews about particular issues with selected groups of adolescents and on the memoirs of their adolescence written by students at the University of Sydney and Sydney Teachers' College. The investigators set out to examine patterns found in how young people in Sydney were handling what were referred to as the 'developmental tasks' of adolescence. Each of these tasks, the authors explained, had a psychological basis. They involved, first, learning appropriate roles; second, achieving emotional maturity; and, third, seeking intellectual maturity. To this list, the authors added 'becoming articulate' later in the book. The responses of youth to their families, friends and peer groups, to radio, films, comic strips, comic books and novels, were discussed in terms of the extent to which they revealed that young people were successfully undertaking these tasks.

The concluding chapter to the book argued that the role of teachers must be to assist the young in making sense of the culture which surrounds them – in being clear about, and able to stand back to analyse, all the social forces that seek to tell them how to lead and interpret their lives. At the same time, they must assist young people in successfully undertaking the developmental tasks of adolescence. These requirements, the authors claimed, suggested four educational tasks as basic to the work of schools and educators dealing with adolescents. To summarize, these were: providing 'the kind of knowledge and skill which is of special value to the adolescent in making a material success of his life'; encouraging young people to use their talents and skills to their full extent; developing their social skills so that they can perceive and execute 'the various roles' they are 'called on to play'; and 'teaching adolescents not merely to participate effectively but to understand and to evaluate the culture which is to become the very fabric of their lives'.[21]

This educational programme was as much a programme for social unity and social order as a means of best serving the individual needs of young people. Developing an understanding of the shared or fundamental social tasks of adolescents and of how young people could be assisted in their achievement would ensure, the authors argued, that despite differences and variations among social groups in the society and from suburb to suburb, there could also be a high level of community of belief and interest. The needs of the social and the individual were contradictory but indeed could and must be made, they insisted, to complement each other.

Connell's study was the most extensive investigation of the lives of Australian youth carried out in the 1950s and 1960s. There were a range of other reports, however, focusing on questions, for instance, of the employment patterns of young people, adolescent uses and responses to the introduction of television and the 'effects' of comics.[22] The latter topic, in particular, provoked a considerable amount of public debate in popular, official and academic contexts. Censorship campaigns in the 1950s claimed that American comics corrupted the minds of Australian children and adolescents. Parents and teachers were called upon to monitor and intervene in the type and number of comics read by young people. As Mark Finnane so clearly shows in his discussion of these debates, what was at stake was the definition of a new social category of youth and the role of various social agencies in the areas of education and welfare in defining and organizing their lives.[23] Australian studies of young people all shared this preoccupation. They described youth as a separate category of person, defined by their vulnerability as they learnt to juggle both their needs as individuals and those of society. Similarly, these studies all insisted that educational and psychological experts should play an expanded role in the lives of young people. In particular, they argued for the importance of drawing on the insights into human development provided by the psychological literature in reforming and establishing new institutions to cater for the 'needs of adolescence'.

The following section discusses a number of key texts of the 1950s that elaborated this argument of the central importance of modern psychological knowledges in reforming the secondary or post-primary education system. It looks at a number of Australian documents produced at different points in the history of this institution, as well as the work of the American psychologist, R.J. Havighurst, whose analysis and recommendations had considerable impact in Australia.

From cultural ideals to normalizing techniques

The concept of adolescence had been established as part of official and academic discourses on education in the 1930s in Australia. ACER published a collection of essays in 1935, edited by Percival Cole, which claimed that this concept was fundamental to the work of those interested in secondary education. Entitled *The Education of the Adolescent in Australia*, these essays set out to reassess the purposes and provisions of secondary education. Written by a number of education officials and experts, they represented, Cole suggested in his introduction, a modest follow-up to the Hadow Report on the education of the adolescent published in Britain in 1926. In the Australian context, they announced the recognition among education professionals that secondary education could no longer be confined to a social elite. The 'old view of education', said Cole, was that 'the classes should have as much of it, and the masses as little as possible'; the new view, that secondary schools should 'embrace and socialize all', acknowledges, he argued, that 'since Nature has provided a period of immaturity and plasticity extending throughout adolescence, no part of this period should be left entirely to the operation of chance influences'.[24]

Adolescence, according to this book, created the need for an extended schooling for all – secondary education for all. This education should cater for the needs of all young people as they undergo the natural process of growing up. But the type of schooling traditionally provided at the secondary level would have to be diversified and adapted to cater for the interests and aptitudes of individual pupils: 'flinging open the door between primary and the secondary school', warned K.S. Cunningham, one of the authors in this collection, would only result in a decline in 'the quality of instruction' provided.[25] The academic, scholastic curriculum of secondary education, previously the unchallenged preserve of a small, socially select section of the population, was not considered appropriate for all young people. Though 'nature', as conceived by the theory of adolescence, might now be recognized to require that all participate in an extended schooling in order to undergo successfully the processes of

(a)

Fig. 1 Monitoring and testing the adolescent: The Child Study Centre. Established in 1956 by Professor O.A. Oeser, a psychologist from the University of Melbourne, this centre was designed to identify children and adolescents supposedly 'at risk'. The photographs show (a) an interview room and (b) an observation room equipped with a one-way mirror.

'normal' growing up, it appeared that she did not require that its traditional curriculum be opened up to the new, non-traditional clientele. 'Nature', this time in the form of 'individual differences', now demanded instead its preservation for an elite, those designated the 'intellectually able' as compared to the 'non-academic adolescents'.

These considerations about the type of education appropriate to the needs of all adolescents prefigured many of the concerns articulated in official and academic discussions of secondary education in the 1950s. During this period, state governments struggled to cope with the massive increase in demand for post-primary education. The schooling system was 'in crisis' throughout the decade with insufficient classrooms and a lack of qualified teachers. But

(b)

secondary education for all began to appear a reality as well as an education policy, initiated, at least in the first instance, not by government action or regulation but by this popular demand. This public interest in increased access to secondary education registered private or family hopes for social mobility.[26] But, these desires were not simply spontaneous; they reflected the greater public attention given to the need for equality of educational opportunity in the years during the war in discussions of the major programmes of social reconstruction planned to take place once the war was over.[27] Yet, conceptualizing secondary education in terms of 'the needs of adolescence' involved a significant reinterpretation of this popular demand. The secondary education to which the broader populace would achieve access in the 1950s and 1960s became a rather different institution to that provided for the privileged few in the decades before the Second World War.

   The intended purpose of a 'democratized' secondary education system, as interpreted by modern psychological knowledges, was to allow young people a moratorium, a space in which they could delay making decisions about what they were going to do with their lives. The Wyndham Report (1957), the report of the committee appointed to review the provision of secondary education in New South Wales, made this point clearly. The predominantly academic curriculum of traditional secondary schools had been designed, it said, 'to serve and reproduce a social as well as an intellectual elite'.[28] Though the clientele entering post-primary education began to broaden early in the twentieth century, policy makers in previous decades, 'untroubled by modern knowledge of the significance of interests and special aptitudes', did not concern themselves with the appropriateness of determining in advance the social and economic futures of young people.[29] 'Modern knowledge', the report intimated, revealed what had in the past not been commonly recognized, that, particularly in the early years of their secondary schooling, adolescents were growing and many of their abilities and interests were nascent. In this new era of greater understanding of the demands of growing up, the challenge for educationists, it concluded, was to meet the needs of all adolescents without impairing the potentialities of any.[30]

In proposing that secondary education should be treated as a space in which young people should have an extended period of time in which to decide who they were and what they wanted to be, the Wyndham Report was by no means suggesting that this space be an unsupervised one. On the contrary, 'modern knowledge' had very particular ideas about how young people should go about making these decisions and using the time made available to them. The 'needs of the adolescent' as interpreted by modern psychological knowledge required that the young person's capacities for shaping the self, making conscious and rational choices about who he or she is, be augmented and nurtured in specific directions. Thus, for example, the Wyndham Report recommended that the organization and the curriculum of the school be designed to facilitate choice, but the requirement to make choices be a progressive one throughout the period of the compulsory years of their secondary education.[31] The moulding and shaping of one's self as a 'choosing self' was to take place according to the developmental norms of adolescent psychology.

The work of American psychologist, R.J. Havighurst, was particularly influential in determining what these norms should be. His ideas on the developmental tasks of adolescence achieved a wide circulation through their dissemination in texts such as W.F. Connell and colleagues' study of Sydney adolescents. They were used widely also in teacher training courses by the late 1950s.[32] According to Havighurst, '[s]chools were created for the sole purpose of helping children to grow up properly'.[33] His book, *Human Development and Education*, first published in 1953, provided an elaborate account of what a proper growing up entailed and how teachers could create the right environment for it to occur.

Havighurst described the history of the concept of the developmental task as he had come to use it. It occupied, he explained,

middle ground between the two opposed theories of education: the theory of freedom – that the child will develop best if left as free as possible, and the theory of constraint – that the child must learn to become a worthy responsible adult through restraints imposed by his society. A developmental task is midway between an individual need and a societal demand. It partakes of the nature of both.[34]

Its value for the educator, he argued, is that it helps first in clarifying the purposes of education – it suggests that the prime purpose of education is to help the individual to achieve certain of these developmental tasks – and, second, it helps determine when to teach various matters – it specifies the 'teachable moment'.[35] Within this framework, the secondary school could become an efficient apparatus in which young people were guided, under the supervisory eye of the teachers, to shape their selves according to the developmental norms Havighurst set out in some detail.

Some tasks, such as learning a masculine or feminine social role, Havighurst suggested, were important at all stages of development. Throughout his book he described what was involved in the successful performance of all of these tasks for each age group from the age of 5 years – the stage, he claimed, when the child became a person and the self began to take a hand in defining the future growth of the individual's personality.[36] But on reaching adolescence, developing personal independence, Havighurst declared, becomes the task which occupies almost all the child's time and energy. This is the stage when 'growth towards autonomy and personal independence' should proceed 'normally to the point where a person becomes independent emotionally, financially, and intellectually'.[37] Carefully planning the learning experience of the child, a detailed knowledge of the developmental tasks of adolescence and their educational implications and the use of such scientific knowledge as sociometric devices to understand the peer culture of pupils, would enable teachers in the modern school, he argued, to produce happy and successful individuals who have achieved their developmental tasks in personally and socially satisfactory ways.

In these terms, the secondary school was to become a carefully regulated environment in which young people learnt to constitute themselves as choosing, self-defining selves. They were to learn the practices of shaping that self and they were to find the desire to become such a self in themselves – in 'the needs of the adolescent'. To become the modern individual could now be a scientific enterprise. Adolescent psychology claimed it could specify in great detail what it meant to be such an individual and how this status could be acquired through the conscientious deployment of its techniques of producing such a self. On the other hand, this science also could specify when things went wrong and why. Havighurst devoted the last section of his book to giving information about case studies of young men and women, of those who failed and those who succeeded. Success depended on the combined and united efforts of family, school and other authorities (such as the church) in guiding the young person through his or her developmental tasks; failure occurred when there was a lack of such assistance.

The purpose of the secondary school was, thus, being massively transformed in the 1950s. Its role was brought more into line with the elementary or primary school, expanding the sphere of public administration whose chief concern is with the shaping of the population.[38] Like the primary school, the secondary school removed children from the unsupervised space of the street to a landscape in which they and their companions could be monitored and their capacities augmented to produce a happy and convinced citizenry – the happy and successful individuals of which Havighurst wrote.[39] Adolescence was constituted as the threshold at which children learnt to take on the social norms 'as one's own'; their individual needs and social responsibilities were said to complement each other through their successfully achieving the developmental tasks as laid down by adolescent psychology. Adolescence as a 'stage' in human development was the time when the individual was to be accustomed, through a set of trainings and material arrangements, to think, act and desire according to a particular set of rules or norms which defined how the self-actualizing individual should operate. Having learnt these particular techniques of acting on the self, the individual was also to learn that the preoccupation with this project of making a self now defined as 'natural' to adolescence was simply 'a stage' in one's development, a stage to be gone through and left behind.

Thus, developmental psychology 'discovered' in the 'nature' of the adolescent, those very needs previously conceived as defining an historically-agreed-upon cultural project. It formulated that ideal as requiring the balancing of societal demands of integration into the social order with the 'need' for the young person to assert an

autonomous, independent sense of self. The developmental task of
the adolescent was to learn to adjust this latter 'need', to reconcile
it with the requirements of the social order. In making these comments, however, I am not concerned to condemn or reject this
human science and associated fields of professional expertise and
educational practice as somehow falsely ideological. I am interested
in how adolescent psychology, through the very defining of its object
– the developing adolescent – and the institutional practices set
up around the classification, monitoring and management of this
category of person, has been productive of its own reality.[40] The
'normal adolescent' (and its counterpart, the pathological or 'delinquent' adolescent) is a historical product of specific social appara-
tuses of regulation and administration, among which the modern
secondary schools play a central role.

I am also interested, however, in how the formulation of the
notion of the modern individual in the norms of adolescent psychology prescribes a set of tasks with particular meanings that limit
the extent to which young women can understand themselves as
wanting, or able, to be such a self. Carol Gilligan, among others, as
I have already shown in Chapter 1, has argued that the image of the
self underlying the norms of developmental psychology is implicitly
gendered. In the following section, I discuss this critique in the
context of the increasing legitimacy of these norms in the modernizing of the Australian secondary education system.

Alternative images of the self?

As indicated in Chapter 1, Gilligan argues that investigations into
the experience of women by Nancy Chodorow, Jean Baker Miller
and herself have identified a different way of imagining the self
than that described by developmental psychology. An image of the
self in relationship, she claims, is characteristic of how women define themselves and their orientation to the world. Other writers
have used Gilligan's work to pursue further the argument that women
operate according to a different definition of selfhood or maturity.
Elizabeth Abel and others in the collection of essays, *The Voyage In:
Fictions of Female Development* (1983), explore this viewpoint in
various studies of what they refer to as the female novel of development – the female *Bildungsroman*. Traditional understandings of
this genre, they claim, have been gender-blind in two ways. First,
they have failed to recognize the way in which the social options
available to young men in their growth to adulthood have not
been equally available to women. In nineteenth-century novels of

formation, for instance, male heroes often pursue their tasks of development in the course of their schooling or by adventures or travel in the outside world. Women could not take advantage of the same experiences as men at this time. These novels celebrated, Abel *et al.* argue, male norms as if they were defining of a universal human experience. Second, they claim, traditional understandings of this genre have not recognized that novels of female development have often shown that women's maturation has inherently different psychological features to that process which is defined as universal or typical. Here they include a discussion of George Eliot's novel, *Mill on the Floss*. Its heroine, Maggie Tulliver, Abel *et al.* suggest, displayed a different set of priorities, a different vision of life, than the one dominant in her society. Her strong allegiance to her parental home, as well as the conflict she experiences between her loyalty to her friend and her passion for her lover, demonstrate a set of considerations and dilemmas which define a developmental path characteristic of female experience.

Fictions of female development, Abel *et al.* claim, reflect the tensions created between the assumptions of a genre in which male norms usually dominate and female protagonists who pursue a different set of values and life orientations. They explain:

> A distinctive female 'I' implies a distinctive value system and unorthodox developmental goals, defined in terms of community and empathy rather than achievement and autonomy. The fully realized and individuated self who caps the journey of the *Bildungsroman* may not represent the developmental goals of women, or of women characters.[41]

The deaths in which these stories so often culminate, they suggest, do not arise from the developmental failures of their heroines but from the difficulty experienced in reconciling these two sets of values; the heroines refuse to accept adulthood as it is currently defined.

These discussions of the gendered character of developmental goals of the fully realized and individuated self appear to raise serious questions about the project of the 1950s adolescent studies and the developmental psychology upon which they drew. W.F. Connell and his colleagues did pay attention to the different experience of growing up available to young men and young women in the early 1950s in Australia. They looked for the differences between the interests and activities of young men and women – differences, for instance, in reading habits, aspirations regarding careers, the desire to travel, enjoyment of physical activities, interest in personal possessions and the importance placed on human relationships. They spoke, too, of young women making choices between a future of a career in the public world or staying at home to raise a family. But they examined these differences within the framework of the developmental tasks of adolescence. In concluding their report, they argued that their study revealed the variety of interests of the young people of Sydney, as well as 'the multiplicity of roles that are played out from time to time'. They went on to say:

> The responses to their social tasks vary, and the problems and satisfactions that each feels most keenly differ from youth to youth and from time to time. The framework of developmental tasks remains the same, but the aspects of them that loom importantly differ from group to group.[42]

Taking on the role of wife and mother, within this analysis, became as much a matter of making choices, deciding who you are and what your life is to be about, as any other choice. The defining characteristic of adolescence for all young people, they asserted, is the possibility of and the need for choosing.[43]

Havighurst similarly wrote of adolescent girls learning to choose, learning to become autonomous, self-defining individuals. They as much as boys, he claimed, have to undertake successfully the developmental tasks of adolescence to achieve a satisfying and happy adult identity. The difference, he maintained, was that, in learning to take on the socially approved feminine role of wife and mother, girls have to accept that they will become economically dependent on a man. But he also noted that society's definition of the feminine role was 'broadening' so that young women who wanted a career – 'girls of this type', as he described them – would find it less difficult in 'adjusting' to social expectations about their futures.[44]

In these analyses of young people written in the 1950s, the tasks of adolescence described a normative set of rules about what a proper growing up entailed. The differences spoken about for young women became simply variations, but the 'needs of adolescence' were supposed to determine their foremost preoccupations. Young women, like young men, were required to learn to be 'choosing selves', if they wanted to attain a certain state of happiness – to become well-adjusted adults. But this literature also represented becoming a housewife and mother or a career woman as choices to be made and to be recognized as such; in making these choices, the individual made herself as well as learnt, as all young people must, to adjust to social expectations.

According to the arguments of Abel *et al.* such claims denied the distinctive way in which young women experience growing up. They attempted to represent as universal, concerns and preoccupations which were not, and are not, relevant to young women. If, however, this literature of the 1950s is understood not as representing – falsely or otherwise – the experience of growing up, but as promulgating vocabularies for understanding and evaluating one's self and one's life, then these issues need to be looked at differently. The texts produced by writers such as Havighurst and Connell and his colleagues disseminated powerful forms of self-understanding. In setting out in detail what a proper growing up should involve, they were establishing a set of normative rules, the role of which was to accustom and train individuals to act, think and desire accordingly. They spoke of particular capacities, of the importance of learning techniques of acting on the self and constituting the self as one's own project. In terms of the discourse of developmental psychology itself, these capacities were interpreted as somehow pre-existing and defining of a human essence – an essence which was to be allowed or assisted to reveal itself – rather than as a cultural ideal. This claim made the normative model of a proper growing up appear all the more powerful, legitimate. As Nikolas Rose remarks more generally about psychological knowledges, their authority stems from the rational discourses of science.[45]

These trainings in themselves were no longer gendered in the 1950s. In the past, young women had mostly been excluded from the social institutions in which these trainings took place. The moves to democratize the secondary education system in the 1950s, however, increasingly ensured that all young people would become subject to the demands and forms of self-evaluation supposedly required of the modern individual. Young women would begin to learn in the modern secondary school that they should want to, and would find pleasure in, making a self and a life for themselves. The choices themselves, however, were still understood in gendered terms. Young women were expected to frame their choices around the decision of whether to become a wife and mother. These were social roles for which young women would now have to find in themselves the desire to undertake, as modern 'choosing selves'.

But the most fundamental sense in which the norms of adolescent psychology were implicitly gendered lay in its counterposing of the needs of the individual and the needs of society. The ideal of the autonomous personality formulated in this context was the individual seeking independence, a defining of the self, separate from social relationships. The social appeared as distinct from the individual, something which he or she had first to resist, only then to become reconciled to in the process of growing up. This was the form of individuality celebrated in the images of modernization as a process of man dominating and controlling the natural and social environment. As Benhabib points out, in elaborating the content of this notion of agency or personhood, Western social and political thought has constituted the world of the feminine by a series of negations around ideas of independence, autonomy, rationality and so on.[46] The following chapters look at other powerful definitions of growing up encountered by young women in the 1950s and early 1960s in the context of the school and elsewhere, and the extent to which they cut across, contradicted or affirmed this gendered formulation of the cultural ideal of the self-determining individual.

5 // The modern school girl: debates about the education of young women

On occasions, such as their retirement, principals of girls' schools in the 1950s often took the opportunity to reflect on how they would define 'the modern school girl'. The terms most frequently used were 'independent', 'mature' and 'well-balanced'. Miss Daniell, for instance, on her retirement as school principal of Ruyton, an exclusive private school in Melbourne, was keen to speak favourably of the 'modern girl'. By the time they left school, 'the present-day girl' was, she said, 'a well-balanced, poised, confident, clear-thinking young woman, capable of doing well almost anything she turned her hand to'. But Miss Daniell's next claim was also typical of how many saw the choices facing the modern young woman in the 1950s. She went on to say, 'Whether it was a career or a marriage and the upbringing of children, she would make a good job of whatever she undertook.'[1]

This chapter looks at some of the major debates about post-primary education in the 1950s and early 1960s in Australia. I examine these debates for what they reveal about the vocabularies available to young women for understanding and evaluating their lives and their futures. I begin by examining the public reports of the 'schooling crisis' mentioned in the previous chapter. Statements about this crisis generally involved considerations of the nature and purpose of a modern schooling. I analyse the changes which occurred during the 1950s in official rhetoric about the role of secondary or post-primary education in young people's lives. I consider whether the debates which arose in this context produced a set of expectations which implicitly or explicitly assumed gender differences in the way in which young people would or should make use of the schooling system. Finally, I look at two features of the educational system of the period to pursue the question of the extent to which young women were being encouraged to think of themselves first and foremost in terms of a sexed identity. I examine the provision of domestic education for girls and I discuss the debates about co-educational schooling. In this chapter, I am concerned to explore the complex and multiple ways in which the subjectivities of young women were shaped in the context of secondary education and, in particular, the way this institution did not address them as gendered identities in any unitary manner.

Modernizing the secondary school system

Writing about Australian schools in the collection of essays, *Australian Civilization*, published in 1962, A.A. Phillips lamented that the modernizing spirit which had gripped the Australian imagination in other arenas in the post-war period had had no impact in the realm of education. This period, he declared,

> should have been a time of rethinking, a time when the revived vigour of Australian energy should have impelled us to shake off our smugness about our schools. The atmosphere of the Australian period which saw the building of the Snowy scheme, the swallowing of over a million migrants, and the dawning recognition that Australia belongs to the Asian hemisphere would have accepted a little creative thinking about the bases of our cultural life ... Our educational administrators should have been drawing the blue prints of a brave post-war world. Instead they were struggling to keep their heads above the floods of kids which swirled about them.[2]

Newspaper reports, parliamentary debates, the yearly reports of educational administrators and statements from teachers' organizations from the early 1950s clearly indicate that the crisis of numbers was the overwhelming preoccupation of all connected with education in this period. The massive growth in the number of young people in post-primary education reflected the high birth rate following the Second World War, the impact of the immigration programme in this same period, and the increasing number of young people staying on at school. Though the minimum leaving age varied from state to state, its significance diminished as young people actively sought an extended schooling.

In the decade 1951–60, enrolments in government primary and post-primary schools increased by 65 per cent and university enrolments rose by 76 per cent. In Victoria in 1959, 80 per cent of young people were staying on at school beyond their fourteenth birthday and just over 60 per cent beyond their fifteenth birthday (the minimum school leaving age in that state at this time was officially 14 years). State secondary or post-primary schools suffered from this growth in numbers; a shortage of classrooms and qualified teachers led to large class sizes and the increased use of temporary buildings. Private schools also experienced a heightened demand for places.[3]

But the crisis for secondary schools was not simply one of numbers. The opening up of post-primary education to all young people meant that the school population had now become more heterogeneous. Pupils came from diverse backgrounds and had a more varied range of expectations of education. Educationists and education officials sought to contain this change by representing it as a problem of what to do about the 'non-academic adolescent'. Particularly in the early 1950s, the new clientele for an extended schooling was defined in terms of an assumed lack of capacity for and interest in the traditional work of the secondary school. In the years immediately following the Second World War, this non-traditional student population received an extended schooling organized basically along the lines set by post-primary education provisions established before the war. For girls, this meant streaming into domestic education or into commercial classes. Education for the female 'non-academic adolescent' was organized according to assumptions about the gendered nature of their needs, destinies and interests. A major ACER study of the educational requirements of Ferntree Gully, an outer suburb of Melbourne, published in 1956, spelt out these expectations. Discussing the educational needs of girls, it turned first to argue for the necessity of domestic education – to 'give *all* of them as high a level of skill as possible in homemaking'. The report also spoke of various occupational destinies for girls and the appropriate form of education required to prepare students for the possibility that they might seek to enter one of these fields. Finally, it outlined the need for education to 'encourage alertness; care in speech, calculation, expression and writing; poise' and to 'provide a proper basis for informed citizenship'.[4] This report demonstrates how in the first half of the 1950s, at least, 'non-academic' girls were understood first and foremost as 'girls'; they were to be prepared for destinies assumed common to and desired by all girls. Education for this population was not to be concerned with developing attributes and skills based on notions of their particular capacities as 'individuals'; they were understood as defined by their sex, and their education was to be organized accordingly. The occupations described for young women reflected the assumption that their lives would follow specific paths appropriate to their sex: clerical work, dressmaking and nursing, for those who wanted to pursue a more extended schooling. The report reflected community expectations about the gendered nature of the vocational destinies of young people in the early 1950s. Yet, at the same time, in their proposals about education of young women, such documents need to be seen as productive of precisely those gendered patterns of achievement, needs and interests.

Similarly, the claim that girls needed training in alertness and poise as part of their general schooling in secondary education pointed to assumptions that their personal attributes should take a gendered form. Although not explicitly speaking of characteristics assumed to be defining of a female presentation of body and self, these orientations or skills were those seen as appropriate, as will become more apparent in Chapter 7, to girls rather than boys. Only the reference to the 'informed citizen' in this instance appeared to make no distinction between how young women and young men should be educated in the modern secondary school.

The streaming of young people into 'academic' and 'non-academic' courses continued throughout the 1950s. Private schools, too, sought to deal with a more diversified student population by giving greater emphasis to subjects which were deemed suitable for girls as 'girls'. Methodist Ladies College in Melbourne, for instance, welcomed the newly introduced Intermediate Certificate in 1944 as benefiting girls who were not 'adapted to academic subjects'. Arts and crafts, dressmaking, domestic science and pre-nursing courses were seen as appropriate to what was now claimed to be a 'multi-purpose school'.[5]

Changes were, however, being mooted in the official educational statements of the latter half of this decade. In some states, such as Victoria, the division (and the associated assumptions about the gendered identities of those deemed 'non-academic') was to be sustained into the 1960s; these assumptions were maintained through the system of differentiated secondary schools deeply entrenched in that state. But at the level of educational rhetoric in the late 1950s, at least, the project of dividing up the population entering the secondary school system on the basis of a claim to know or be able to predetermine their capacities for and interest in the traditional academic work of these schools began to be made problematic. The report of the committee appointed to review state education in Victoria (the Ramsay Report), for instance, advised that explicit vocational choice for young people be deferred until the age of 15 years. Though they stepped back from making recommendations that would have drastically altered the system of post-primary schooling in that state, they urged that the current arrangement be made flexible enough to allow students to transfer from one type of school to another. The problem was, they argued, that:

> We are assured that it is not possible, by any known device, to allocate children fairly to particular types of study at the age of twelve, although one can, with some certainty, predict what the level of performance will be in some studies requiring intelligence, providing motives remain the same.[6]

While this committee expressed a continued commitment to the reliability of measures of intelligence as a way of differentiating the population entering post-primary schooling, other bodies were casting doubt on the appropriateness of any claims to be able to know the student population in this or any form. In its more far-reaching and radical reassessment of secondary schooling in New South Wales, the Wyndham Committee also pointed to the significance of interest and motivation in determining the paths taken by students once they entered secondary school, factors which could not be predicted before they embarked on this stage of their education. But they cast doubt, too, on the value of any measures which claimed to be able to determine levels of general intelligence such as the IQ test. During adolescence, needs, interests and abilities manifest themselves, they claimed, which were not evident in individuals at the beginning of this period of their life. They advocated a general, comprehensive form of schooling for all students in order to facilitate the best environment for all types of aptitudes and talents to manifest themselves.[7]

In the educational literature of this period promulgating the theories of adolescent psychology, the argument for a general rather than specialized or vocationally oriented education in the early years of secondary education was based on the notion of the developmental needs of the individual. These ideas, as shown in the discussion of the Wyndham Report in the previous chapter, received support in official government documents and reports. However, such reports were also particularly concerned with 'the needs of society', the 'need' for social integration. Extended schooling for the whole population of young people, they claimed, was crucial in the production of a modern citizenry. In this supervised space, the young could be led to take on the social norms as 'one's own', to become the self-regulating individual who is at the same time a happy member of the social group (the 'convinced citizen' in Franco Moretti's terms).[8] Rather than being an institution simply preoccupied with preparing young people for specific destinations, whether it be university or particular occupations, the secondary school was now to be a space in which all aspects of a young person's life could be monitored and directed according to the norms considered appropriate to producing this modern citizenry. In this context, teachers could no longer rely on simply teaching particular subjects; they must, in the words of the Wyndham Report, recognize the secondary school's 'responsibility for the pastoral care and guidance of its pupils'.[9] All aspects of the young person's life were to be brought into the arena of the secondary school: physical and emotional health, mental skills and capacities, readiness for group membership, the ability to communicate, preparedness to enter the world of work, spiritual values, and the ability to use one's leisure time in 'a profitable and satisfying fashion'.[10] Ian Hunter has discussed the way in which the primary school in the early twentieth century increasingly became a 'norm-saturated environment'.[11] The secondary school in the post-war period was to take on this character as its purpose shifted increasingly away from its earlier function of the preparation of particular populations for specific futures to the role of producing this modern citizenry in whom all these characteristics had been instilled.

According to official and popular rhetoric about education in the 1950s, augmenting the capacities of young people to 'think for themselves' was essential to the well-being of both the individuals themselves and society. In the early years of this decade in particular, such rhetoric emphasized the needs of democracy, and the spectre of the Second World War became a warning about the fragility of this ideal of the democratic way of life. To meet the challenges which had been and were continuing to be posed to that way of life, teachers should, said Mr Ramsay, the Director of Education in Victoria, 'produce thinking citizens, ones who could sort the grain from the chaff; unselfish citizens and self-disciplined citizens'. But at the same time, he added, this focus on citizenship must not be pursued at the cost of individuality. 'We no longer spoke of moulding children', he reassured his audience.[12] To achieve this balance the secondary school was, thus, to encourage self-discipline instead of imposing an 'old-fashioned', 'authoritarian' discipline. Rather than 'mould' children, schools were to teach pupils to take on the supervisory gaze of the teacher for themselves and to become self-governing.

References to the nature of 'modern society' also served to support these claims about the need for schools to focus on producing a modern citizenry. '[M]odern industrialised civilization' requires, stated one newspaper leader article on education, that modern schools develop techniques and approaches which are social and cooperative, rather than foster the atmosphere of 'old-time discipline', if students are to acquire 'a sense of responsibility and social duty'.[13] The complexity of the modern world, new political and economic conditions, the rapidity of social change and technological developments, according to this type of claim, necessitated a new type of education in which all young people could learn to take an active part in this world as modern citizens.

By the late 1950s, a new emphasis had appeared in statements about the role of the secondary school in producing this modern citizenry. This rhetoric was now just as likely to be preoccupied with the extent to which young people had received sufficient training in scientific and technological skills. The 'modern' in this context required that an extended system of schooling increase the levels of scientific knowledge in the community as a whole, as well as encourage more of the 'talented few' to undertake scientific or technologically oriented careers. The traditional was now constituted not in the image of a different style of schooling, but in terms of the content of education. The humanities became 'the traditional', or at best, secondary to the modern – the domestic handmaiden ensuring that scientists and technologists remain humanized.

In the early 1950s, advocates of an increased emphasis on scientific education had drawn on the language of 'the modern' as a way of creating a sense of excitement about science. Science symbolized the modern: it was progress, adventure, 'an attack on the unknown', the desire to 'discover the marvelous pattern of a perfect universe'.[14] By the mid-1950s, the voices of scientists such as Mark Oliphant, Ian Clunies-Ross and Harry Messel increasingly began to be heard in the daily press, but their statements made a different use of the image of modernity. Now it became a matter of Australia losing its place in the modern world if it continued to pay insufficient attention to science and the scientific training of its population. Science became synonymous with the modern.

Scientists began pointing to Russian supremacy in space research and technological education as a means of creating a sense of urgency about their claims. The 'free world', or Western 'democracies', had been left behind, they warned.[15] This nation which had been constituted increasingly in the years after the Second World War as the 'Other' of the project of modernity – as the place of authoritarianism, darkness, co-option and rigidity rather than democracy, freedom and the progress of the individual and society – had overtaken the Western world in the very field it had used to symbolize the modern. When Russia launched its satellite, *Sputnik 1*, and its path across Australian skies could be constantly monitored and reported in the daily press in October 1957, advocates of increased scientific education finally had a symbol which could be clearly used to capture the popular imagination and galvanize educational administrators, business people and politicians into taking concrete action. In 1957, the Prime Minister, Robert Menzies, announced that the federal government would stimulate the development of Australian universities and, in particular, the areas of basic science in those institutions. The Murray Committee, formed in that same year to review the system of university education, recommended that the first faculties to be established in Melbourne's second university (what was to become Monash University) be in the areas of the pure sciences, engineering and technology.

In New South Wales, the state parliament debated how to encourage more students to study science.[16] The Wyndham Committee in that state paid particular attention, too, to the need for all young people to receive a certain level of scientific and mathematical education in their recommendations about a common curriculum. They resisted pressure from those making submissions to the committee who attempted to persuade them that the growing demands of scientific and technological knowledge required that the focus of science teaching in the schools should be on identifying those with talent in its various fields and cultivating their skills as quickly as possible. Instead, they viewed science education in the secondary school as crucial to its role in producing a modern citizenry. There were, they claimed, 'certain fields of thought and experience of which no adolescent should be ignorant as a person or a citizen'.[17]

The levels of resources and teaching in the fields of science and mathematics subjects slowly began to improve and change in state and private schools. In 1959, a fund was established 'for the advancement of scientific education in schools'. Established on behalf of a number of industrial and commercial organizations and modelled on a similar body in Britain, it set out to collect funds to build high-quality science laboratories in 'boys' schools of standing'.[18] The focus of the Industrial Fund on elite boys' schools received some criticism in the daily press for its exclusion of government schools and non-government girls' schools. Its project was made redundant in 1964, with the introduction by Menzies of a federal government programme to fund science laboratories and facilities in state and private schools.[19]

In their concern to promote greater interest in science and technology and to encourage more young people to specialize in these fields, public spokesmen at times pointed to the absence of young women in appropriate secondary school and higher education courses. Often, claims in terms such as the 'wastage of talent' in-cluded references to young 'men and women'. At other times, more specific references were made to the importance of attracting young women into these areas as a way of dealing with the problem of the shortage of trained scientists, engineers, technicians, science teachers and so on. Ian Clunies-Ross complained in 1956 that girls' schools had not 'paid any great attention to science in the past'.[20] Harry Messel accused the community of ordaining that women should lead a life of 'terrible scientific illiteracy' by the way in which 'any girl who showed an interest in physics, mathematics or other branches of science was sneered at, laughed at and looked upon as an oddity'.[21]

The more general tenor of the call for a scientifically trained population, however, suggested that it was the young men who were sought. The Australian scientists quoted above, the scientific researchers, the university leaders and administrators, and the young 'brains' pictured handling great machines and complicated tech-nology, were all men. It was the 'young schoolboys' who were spoken about as thrilling to the 'excitement' and 'adventure' of science and space travel, just as it was the 'budding boy scientists' whose school experiments were reported in newspaper articles on science talent searches.[22] This gendering of the scientist and the areas of science education worked to suggest that such activities were not for girls. They were not the prime targets addressed by publicity which sought to enhance the sense of excitement to be had in the world of sci-ence. The language of scientific research – 'reaching outwards to the edge of the universe', struggling with nature (putting questions to her so that 'she' cannot 'wriggle out of it') and avoiding 'ethical and emotional conclusions in their work'[23] – suggested a set of capacities and orientations which described the masculine, not the feminine. Bodies such as the Wyndham Committee may have desired a more scientifically trained population as a whole, but these images ap-peared to suggest that it was appropriate that young men, rather than young women, pursue achievement or success in this arena.

Yet the image of educational achievement itself in this period did not necessarily exclude girls. The rhetoric about the role of educa-tion in producing a modern citizenry made no distinctions between the educational activities to be provided for young men and young women. Similarly, phrases like 'the wastage of talent' or the 'abilities of individuals' could also be inclusive of young women, not by any explicit concern to do so, but by their apparent neutrality. A sub-mission from the Headmistresses' Association of New South Wales to the Wyndham Committee examining secondary education in that state demonstrates this point. Representing 27 independent girls' schools, this association made statements to the committee on a range of issues concerned with post-primary education. Yet there was little in this document to indicate that this was a group of women talking about the education of girls. Though they did mention domestic science subjects and referred explicitly on occasion to the 'education of girls', their central preoccupations were articulated in the language of 'talent', 'every level of ability', a 'wide range of choice for the individual' and the need to train students 'in the essential skills, to develop this power of independent thought and reasoning'.[24]

Jill Ker Conway's autobiography, *The Road to Coorain*, indicates that at least some young women did precisely manage to understand themselves as interpellated by the vocabularies of 'educational achievement' circulating around and within the space of the secondary school in the 1950s and early 1960s. As a young woman, she understood her life and self as organized, made meaningful and pleasurable by the educational identity.

In making this claim, however, I do not intend to ignore the significance of the vast differences in the levels of educational participation of young men and women in this period. Norman Mackenzie, in his investigation into the situation of women in Australia, published in 1962, lamented the higher rate of loss of young women from all types of schools and all ages compared to men. Eighty out of every 1,000 boys in government schools, he pointed out, were still at school on their seventeenth birthday, whereas only 47 out of every 1,000 girls had survived. Girls, he concluded:

> ... are slipping out of school more rapidly than the boys, year by year, and more than half of them leave between 14 and 15. By the time the point is reached where a girl can seriously consider whether she wants some special post-secondary training, such as preparation for nursing, teaching or a commercial course – let alone a university degree – relatively few are still left at school. Even in 1960 only 16 out of every 1,000 starters reached this level, and for each year one goes back the proportion becomes smaller.[25]

The type of schooling received and the use made of it by different groups of young people continued to be determined very profoundly, as the figures quoted by Mackenzie demonstrate, by class and gender factors. Yet, the simple fact of the expansion of the secondary education system, with the vast majority of the population now receiving some form of extended schooling, had its own major effects. It ensured that all young people began to experience 'youth' itself. They were to participate in an institution which increasingly defined them as a separate category of person with special needs and interests. They were also to participate in an institution which claimed that, as 'youth', they had both the opportunity and obligation to make a self and a life for themselves. And the form in which the school told them it was most appropriate and desirable to make that self, was through educational achievement and success. Conway's autobiography indicates that for at least a minority of young women, this understanding of the self offered an important and pleasurable sense of identification. For others, structural impediments remained, both in terms of social background and type of education offered to them, preventing a great many from feeling at home with the education system's claim to provide the tools and opportunity to undertake this making of a self. The project of the modernized secondary school, however, was to shape the aspirations and the evaluations of one's life and self of all young people in accordance with its claim about the necessity of them all becoming modern individuals.

Schooling and the achievement of a sexed identity

A different set of practices in the secondary education system, however, recruited this notion of making a self to an affirmation of a normative definition of femininity. Official and popular representations of the training of girls in preparation for the roles of wife and mother in this period claimed that these practices gave young women the benefits of the 'modern'. In this instance, the modern involved the systematization and augmentation of the skills and attributes of the housewife and mother, but the recognition too of these capacities as achievements. Through domestic education, the modern young woman could make herself in feminine form.

Newspaper reports paid public tribute to this story of female achievement. In the *Sydney Morning Herald* of November 1953, the following report appeared:

> *'I Made it Myself!' Schoolgirls Stage a Dress Parade*
> The wide lawns in front of the Parramatta Home Science Secondary School – built on the site of a former home of Samuel Marsden – made an unusual background for a mannequin parade yesterday at the school.
> The models were not the familiar willowy mannequins who look from the glossy pages of high fashion magazines, but the

15-year-old intermediate students of the school, dressed in frocks they made themselves as part of their sewing course this year.

Nearly all the girls chose cotton materials – pastel shaded linens, bright everglaze and cotton shantungs – for the dresses which they cut from patterns draughted at sewing classes during the year. Classrooms were transformed into dressing rooms for the parade, and when girls emerged in the school corridors in their pretty dresses, high-heeled shoes and lipstick – instead of the baggy tunic – teachers commented, 'Well they all look at least three years older!'[26]

A local newsreel in July 1953 also provided a similar report of such an event. Film had the advantage of being able to show the transformation of marching girls in their 'baggy tunics' into young women floating around rose gardens, gracefully pointing their toes and presenting their clothes, and themselves, to be admired.[27]

These reports demonstrate many of the themes central to this particular story of female achievement. It is an account of the ritual of a young woman's 'coming out' as she demonstrated her capacities to produce her body in feminine form. It celebrated her metamorphosis from schoolgirl in unsexed tunic to a sexed identity of a feminized bodily existence in 'pretty clothes' and of 'mature' appearance. The young woman presenting herself in this school mannequin parade had made not just her own clothes, but her 'self'. But the mention of cotton in the newspaper report was significant. Cotton frocks or cotton swimsuits in such contexts spoke of a practical and demure femininity. School girls taking on a sexed identity through the wearing of sensible cotton and pastel colours demonstrated a carefully managed femininity, a femininity-under-control. Although such accounts of the teaching of the skills of being able to make one's clothes to young women always presented this education as providing girls with the benefits of 'the modern', it was also assumed that they would use these skills to produce themselves according to the dictates of such a femininity. The public space provided for a feminine presence, both by such reports as these, and by the girls' schools they spoke of, recruited the story of growing up in the modern world to the affirmation of this normative definition of femininity.

In the late 1950s, in the context of arguments opposing the streaming of young people too early in their secondary education, some educators began to argue that all girls should receive some form of

Fig. 2 Making a self – in feminine form (from the *Sydney Morning Herald*, 12 December 1957). The caption under the schoolgirl photograph shown here also illustrates the everydayness of a particular form of racism in this period.

domestic education. Through the rituals and practices of domestic education, the secondary school of the 1950s and 1960s was involved in mapping a particular terrain as the feminine. Just as the secondary school had become a space in which education administrators and psychologists sought to extend and elaborate the techniques of pastoral surveillance to produce a modern citizenry of self-governing individuals, so too had it become a space designed to produce a set of attributes in certain sections of the population as defining and necessary to the feminine. Wherever girls are taught, said the Ramsay Report, describing the provisions of the 1958 Education Act in Victoria, it is ensured that the 'practical and theoretical instruction in domestic arts' is given.[28] The practices and rhetoric of secondary education constituted femaleness as a shared identity for young women in this form of a common destiny, and hence, common needs.

Thus arguments for the necessity of domestic education for all young women in this period rested on these claims about their common destinies. These had been articulated in a most detailed form in a British report by John Newsom, *The Education of Girls*, published in 1948. Though he insisted that there were 'marked physiological and psychological differences' between men and women, Newsom also claimed that his major concern was to provide young women with an education which prepared them for the socially determined roles they would play in a 'civilized community'. For 'the vast majority of women', he said, 'the business of home-making and the early nurture of children is a dominant theme in their lives'.[29] Newsom made elaborate claims about the skills required of the 'successful homemaker and mother'. He praised, among other things, her technical skills of cookery, home nursing, her abilities in the management of resources and as teacher of the young, her knowledge of psychology, her artistic skills as homemaker, and her personal qualities of patience, humour, courage and resilience.[30]

Newsom was elaborating the skills and personal qualities to be taught in the secondary school to young women. These were attributes to be learnt to enable women to achieve success and satisfaction in their 'careers' as housewives and mothers. Systematizing and augmenting the capacities designated feminine in this way, worked to suggest that young women should understand themselves first and foremost as 'girls', and as having a shared destiny and identity in this form. Newsom's tone was patronizing, despite his insistence on placing great value on these competencies. Yet his arguments point to the way domestic training in the school was about producing capacities; it was about developing and enhancing the competencies of the housewife and mother. In his reworking of Donzelot's arguments about the modern family, Jeffrey Minson suggests that the institutionalization of domestic education for young women should be seen as an important basis for women's historical emancipation. The 'creation of an agent, the housewife, whose "career" and newfound rights, powers and responsibilities', he says, 'are created by the valorisation of tasks in respect to a domain of the domestic', does not strip women of their rights but, on the contrary, produces a role with associated powers and rights. This power carries with it its own burdens, but it does also provide women with a position from which to speak, a position from which to speak about having special knowledge on certain topics, and about having needs and rights.[31] These processes themselves were not oppressive of women in the sense of necessarily subordinating or repressing capacities which would have otherwise been allowed to express themselves as 'naturally' present in all persons.[32] Similarly, domestic education needs to be seen as constituting a particular form of agency with associated powers and responsibilities for young women.

The disadvantages experienced by young women in the education system, in relationship to this particular issue, were two-fold. The first problem lay in the way in which practices such as timetabling and streaming assumed that it was appropriate to exclude young women from other sets of trainings provided in the school. In this sense, they were to be arranged under the category of their sex and their education organized accordingly.[33] Second, domestic education, as I indicated earlier in this chapter, had been the form of secondary education given to those designated as non-academic in the early 1950s – to those considered as not properly belonging in the secondary school. In this manner, a gendered identity had become the only form in which a large number of young women in the setting of the school could have a sense of achievement, a sense of being able to make themselves. With the moves to provide a comprehensive system of schooling which no longer streamed young people rigidly according to such categories by the mid-1950s, the argument that all young women should receive domestic education began to be put into practice in the first year or so of their secondary schooling, but this earlier sense of its place did not thereby immediately disappear. Requiring all young women to undertake some form of domestic education intimated that their status was uncertain or limited in the secondary school.

The practices and policies of domestic education worked to suggest, that for young women, the affirmation of sexual difference meant the acceptance of their specific destinies as wife and mother. To

Fig. 3 Wives and mothers to be: 'Modern' education for girls in the 1950s. A new domestic science classroom, Newcastle 1956.

understand oneself as female in the context of the modern secondary school required an understanding of the self in these terms. The shift from providing domestic education for a specific group of 'non-academic' female adolescents to its inclusion in the education of all girls signalled a shift to this centrality of the roles of wife and mother in defining the 'essential feminine' in the context of the school. In the early 1950s, domestic education had been provided to a limited group of non-traditional clientele of the secondary school. Its role at this time reflected the way the education system had clearly been a class-based social institution before the Second World War. A policy of domestic education for all girls, rather than making these explicit class differentiations among the population of young people entering secondary school, worked to produce a unified category of young women with shared concerns and destinies. I have also argued in this chapter, however, that young women encountered other vocabularies about the self and about one's place in the world – other identities – through their increasing participation in the education system in the 1950s and 1960s. These alternative constructions of the self worked against the suggestion that a sense of one's self as a sexed identity should define the essential truth of who one is and what life should be about.

Moves to establish comprehensive, co-educational schools in the 1950s constituted another arena in which the terms of sexual difference were being defined and reworked. Debate about the desirability of co-education became most heated in the context of the Wyndham Committee's deliberations about the future shape of the secondary school system in New South Wales. A number of submissions were made to the committee in support of co-education; newspaper reports of their views sparked letters to the editor from supporters and opponents. The committee in its final report presented a moderate view, recommending that, in the future, schools be co-educational. They pointed out, however, that there was no conclusive evidence that this type of education was in all ways better for young people. Newspaper reports indicated that the committee itself was not unanimous on this issue.[34] Its recommendations were made in the context of providing a comprehensive system of schooling which would not force young people to make premature decisions about their futures.

Yet, the main concerns articulated in this debate were of a different nature. Advocates and opponents chiefly addressed the issue of whether or not this type of educational arrangement produced a more 'natural' relationship between the sexes. 'The child normally exists in a mixed society,' declared a submission from the staff of one high school, 'and the school acting as a miniature society enables boys and girls to develop together under supervision, learning to react normally and naturally to each other.' Claiming overwhelming support from staff and most parents of children at the school, this submission set out arguments predominantly concerned with the social benefits of a system, as they saw it, in which young people would not grow up as 'segregated strangers'.[35]

Similar statements were made by advocates of co-education in the popular press. 'Co-educational schools', they insisted, 'trained boys and girls for real life.' 'The school atmosphere and personal relationships between pupils and staff are usually much healthier and happier', claimed a teacher writing of her experiences in both single- sex and country co-educational schools. And a women teachers' organization was reported as believing that when girls and boys work together in a school '[e]ach develops a sane attitude towards the opposite sex'.[36] These arguments spoke of students as sexual identities. The purpose of co-education in their terms was to create a space in which those identities could be produced, monitored and regulated according to norms of what was 'normal' and 'natural'. A letter claiming to quote the American psychologist, Dr Kinsey, illustrates this point clearly. The writer asserted that when Kinsey was asked if he preferred sex-segregated or co-educational schools, he replied 'You mean do I prefer homosexual or heterosexual schools?' The letter continued:

> Co-educational schools, because they naturally suggest that the human is composed of males and females who are equally important in the scheme of things, are an aid in fostering a balanced social and emotional maturity in the adult-to-be. They provide opportunity . . . for the young of both sexes to become aware of each other and understand each other as a natural and important part of their education and growing up.[37]

According to such claims, secondary education should ensure that young people identify themselves as sexed creatures with appropriate and correctly managed sexual desires for 'the opposite sex'. Such identities were seen as central to what the young were about. School dances, school productions such as plays and concerts, and sports carnivals provided spaces in which, under the supervision of teachers, they could learn to understand themselves thus. Co-education was not about treating all students as the same or as 'neuters', but, on the contrary, its purpose was to attempt to ensure that 'natural' heterosexual desires were incited and managed in the correct manner. Co-education, it was claimed, would lower the divorce rate.[38]

Opponents of co-education, on the other hand, insisted that such educational arrangements would incite too much interest in the opposite sex. The issue at stake revolved around how best to regulate the sexual identities of students and the function of the school in this process. Opponents of co-education asserted that the presence of the 'opposite sex' would mean that they would distract each other. A 'child specialist' was quoted in the *Sydney Morning Herald* as doubting claims that co-education promoted 'social adjustment between the sexes'; she suggested instead that 'the inevitable results' would be 'earlier marriage or increased promiscuity, both of which increase the divorce rate'. This result was inevitable, she said, 'because nature is nature and sex is sex, and immature emotions plus mature bodies . . . have inevitable results'.[39]

Single-sex or segregated schools, their supporters were quick to point out, did not produce young people who were socially or emotionally stunted. '[T]he other sex is not at all disregarded', claimed one letter to the press. 'Most High Schools, both State and Church, have their "sister" schools and organise joint social functions.'[40] Another argued that girls were 'more ladylike, more gentle, less tough and more feminine' when educated apart from boys in their adoles-

cence.[41] These schools ensured that their students were produced as
sexed identities, but this was to be achieved through different means
than those seen as appropriate by co-educational schools. Awareness
of one's identity in these terms would be incited by social occasions
with the opposite sex, just as the single sex atmosphere would ensure
that gendered attributes could be produced with greater ease.

Thus both sides in the debate understood the adolescent as a
sexual identity. Although they disagreed about the best way to regulate and supervise that identity, there was a general consensus that
adolescence was a period in life when this sexuality should be incited, monitored and chanelled in 'natural' and socially desirable
directions. In this sense, education was an important site for defining
the terms of sexual difference around a powerful sense of one's
self as a sexual identity. That identity was considered 'naturally' a
heterosexual one in which 'natural' and 'normal' desires were to be
recognized, but also managed and contained; adolescence was about
preparing oneself for heterosexual maturity, for marriage. For young
women, in this context, the affirmation of their femaleness meant
the acceptance of this construction of the self as a sexualized identity. In a co-educational school, the student would be trained to take
on the supervisory gaze of the teacher to learn to manage one's
sexuality; in the single-sex school, sexual impulses were to be contained, held back until maturity would enable the young person to
regulate them in appropriate ways.

Through the practices and rhetoric concerned with domestic education and co-education or single-sex education, then, the secondary
school of the 1950s was playing a constitutive role in the formation
of young women as sexed and sexual identities. This institution
sought to shape the personal investments of young women in such
a way that they would evaluate their lives and actions according to
their sense of how well they managed to operate in accordance with
these norms. But this institution also made available, as I argued
in the previous section, other vocabularies which were presented as
fundamental to how all young people should evaluate their lives.
In the previous chapter, I looked at the discourse of adolescent
psychology in these terms. In this chapter, I have suggested that the
educational rhetoric and practices devised around notions of 'the
needs of democracy' and the vocabularies and techniques of making
a self, promulgated by the notions of educational attainment competed with notions of one's sexed identity as the supposed key to
the truth of one's self in the context of the modernized secondary
school. The needs and aspirations of young women were being shaped
in complex and multiple ways in this institutional setting.

6 / Youth on the streets: the social regulation of young people as 'teenagers' and as 'youth'

The expansion of the secondary schooling system in the 1950s and early 1960s both constituted and gave public visibility to a new social identity. The rhetoric about the necessity of an extended education for all represented young people as a social group needing time-out, a space in which to make a self. This space was to be carefully monitored and regulated by teachers and educational experts. The supervision of this space of the adolescent schoolchild, according to the educational and psychological discourses elaborated at this time, was designed to ensure they became convinced citizens ready to assume membership of a modern democratic nation. As citizens-in-the-making, they were dependent on their adult mentors for guidance and for the organization of appropriate spaces in which they could grow up properly.

Other agencies and institutions at this time, however, spoke of young people in different terms. The category of the 'teenager', in advertising and popular culture contexts in this period, frequently constituted the young as economic citizens. In this form, they were represented as already active members of the society and were given a voice in these terms. Official and media reports referring to 'teenagers', however, were as much interested in defining the responsibilities of parents in managing the adolescence of their children, as in addressing the concerns of young people themselves. In this chapter, I look at the category of the teenager. In particular, I discuss the way this category constituted young people as a significant social group and at the tensions articulated through and around its usage as a public form of address. I then turn to examine official and media statements about 'the problem of juvenile delinquency' as another context in which the responsibilities of parents in relationship to their adolescent children were delineated. Finally, in this chapter, I look at the activities of youth on the streets – at those outside or threatening adult authority, as well as those firmly placed within this sphere – in the forms of 'the teenage fan', 'organized youth' and 'student protesters', and discuss the issues which emerged in media representations of these public identities. I am interested in how all these definitions of youth both augmented this period in young people's lives and provided powerful definitions of how they should understand and experience the process of their growing up.

The teenager

A study of working girls, *Girls Growing Up*, published in England in 1942, lamented that they turned to the cinema and to dancing to escape the dreary monotony of their working lives. But these young women had little to spend on their entertainment or material needs. The study reported that they gave their wages to their parents, keeping only a small amount of pocket money for themselves. Even after they had been working for a couple of years, their possessions consisted of basic items of clothing and perhaps a few fashion accessories or trinkets. The young women studied reported enjoying the independence of having a job, although their desires to express that independence seemed to be modest.[1]

By 1959, a quite different picture emerged in a document, entitled *The Teenage Consumer*, prepared by Mark Abrams. According to Abrams, British youth had been newly enfranchised 'in an economic sense' since the Second World War. Unencumbered by house mortgages and other financial obligations, paying only a small amount of board to parents, 'the nation's 4,200,000 working teenagers', Abrams declared,

> ... dispose of roughly £17 millions a week of uncommitted spending power – or £850 millions a year. To this latter figure we can add another £50 millions as the amount received as pocket money by the 800,000 nonemployed teenagers – making a grand total of £900 millions a year to be spent by teenagers at their own discretion.[2]

Abrams went on to discuss the characteristics of this 'uncommitted spending power', arguing that a distinctive pattern of teenage spending could be identified – 'distinctive teenage spending for distinctive teenage ends in a distinctive teenage world'.[3] Manufacturers, he declared, would have to learn to take account of the particular features of this market.

In Australia by the late 1950s, young people were receiving a great deal of public visibility as the target of marketing strategies of domestic and overseas manufacturers keen to take advantage of their new spending power. No such document as the one prepared by Abrams seems to have appeared in this country, but several articles in the *Sydney Morning Herald* noted that the level of demand for juvenile labour, as well as the rapid growth of the teenage population itself, meant that the teenage market in Australia was increasingly becoming 'big business'. As Abrams recorded in the British context, a feature article in 1957 drew attention to what it characterized as the uninhibited character of teenage spending. Free of worries about mortgages and the necessity of repairing the washing machine, teenagers, the article declared, have 'time to become good shoppers'. They are cash buyers, it claimed, and spend most of their money on themselves. It noted, too, differences between the spending habits of males and females: teenage girls, the article suggested, spent little on entertainment (relying on their boyfriends to pay), but considerable amounts on make-up and clothes; teenage boys purchased gramophone records, sporting gear and clothes.[4]

The affluence of this teenage market had obviously been recognized by commercial interests in Australia before 1957. But it was only clearly identified in this form a few years earlier – as a 'teenage market' – and, at times, the spending power of young people continued to be understood in different ways. For instance, commercial radio in the 1950s initiated specific programmes for 'teenagers', frequently compered by 'teenage announcers', yet in their appeals to potential advertisers they often used different ways of identifying their audience of young people. These commercial interests were recognizing and shaping a new consumer identity, while also persisting with other forms of identification which cut across this new category. Material from a trade journal for the broadcasting industry exemplifies this point. Promoting the advantages of advertising on commercial radio, the Australian Federation of Commercial Broadcasting Stations published a statement in the magazine, *Broadcasting and Television*, in 1957, dividing their claimed audience of 'millions' into three categories: women, men and children. Of its largest audience, women, the advertisement announced:

> They're mothers, grandmothers, young wives and single girls.
> They're the planners of the nation's shopping lists, today's
> and tomorrow's home-makers. They're society women, house-
> wives, typists, waitresses, wives, factory workers and ballet girls.
> They're women from every job – every occupation but they
> have one thing in common . . . THEY BUY RADIO ADVERTISED GOODS.[5]

While this category of 'women' included young female workers, their category of 'children' included the young male workers: the 'office boys, apprentices, junior clerks, messengers . . .'. Young people at high schools and colleges also appeared under this latter heading. 'Children' were not so much consumers in their own right, according to this document, as those who influenced the family's buying and were 'tomorrow's adult consumers'. Later that same year, however, this same journal published the results of a study it had conducted on 'young people's preferences'. The category 'teenager' was used in this instance and included young male and female workers, apprentices and university students.[6]

This material shows how commercial interests sought to address young women in the 1950s both as 'women' and as 'teenagers'. As forms of self-identification, they intimated different notions of the problems and possibilities of the personal investment at stake in being a consumer. As 'women', young women had, either now or in the future, both the power and responsibility of being in charge of the consumption activities of others. In the purchasing of goods for themselves, their responsibility was also to buy for others – to please and to make themselves desirable for others. As 'teenagers', on the other hand, they were without responsibility; spoken of as in a limbo world between childhood and adulthood, they found themselves increasingly courted in this form by these interests eager to persuade them to purchase in precisely this way – as autonomous and as concerned only with pleasing themselves.[7]

Through such rhetoric, then, commercial interests speaking to 'the teenager' constituted young people as having some form of citizen status. As 'teenagers', they had both a public visibility and a public importance. They were provided with an identity which proclaimed them able to act in the world, to be independent agents and to act on their own desires and wishes. So, too, were they defined as having their own voice, to which the attentive marketplace listened and responded. This enfranchisement was limited, but significant nevertheless. It represented a major change from understanding oneself according to the category of the 'child'. This latter identification speaks of dependency, of a declared inability as well as a social prohibition against acting autonomously. For young women, its significance was even greater as they acquired a form of self-identification which spoke of their independence, their capacity for autonomous action and their ability to be self-defining. Thus, advertisements appealing to 'teenagers', 'teenage girls' or in terms like 'Miss teens' encouraged young women to consider themselves as in charge not only of their own money but of their lives and identities.

Young people had been the targets of advertising before the Second World War. In the American context, Stuart Ewen suggests that children in the 1920s and 1930s were often responsible for pushing their families to expand the level of consumption in the home. They were a conduit, he argues, for the new commercial culture.[8] But the growing levels of affluence throughout the population and the buoyancy of the labour market for young people in the 1950s gave them increased independent spending power. As Jill Blackmore notes in the Australian context, a relatively high demand for juvenile labour was at least part of the reason why the long-term pattern of early school leaving continued throughout the 1950s. Work, not school, she suggests, was the norm for young people in the age group 15–19 years during this period. These trends continued into the early 1960s. Extreme shortages were most notable in the areas of employment for young women. They were primarily employed in the areas of commerce, finance, property, education and health. The demand for young women was highest in the occupations requiring cheap, unskilled labour, but a marked shortage in the more skilled occupations such as nursing and banking also existed.[9]

Both public and private employers initiated recruitment drives to attract young people. Wage incentives were offered as were various promises about the modern and attractive features of working conditions. Appeals to young women to consider nursing as a career, for instance, spoke in glowing terms of the new, 'modern' living quarters provided for trainees – 'a home away from home' – and the excellent potential such a career offered in terms of opportunities for travel and excitement.[10] Similarly, banks advertised their 'well-paid positions' for 'young ladies', drawing attention to the lifestyle benefits and social activities offered in their 'modern' buildings.[11]

Sought after, then, by employers and by commercial interests, young people – and young women in particular – were constituted as a public identity in quite different terms to those promoted by the notion of adolescence. The latter portrayed young people as in need of supervision and monitoring. It made problematic those who left school early – those young workers these other interests were so eager to attract – as potentially at risk in making a 'normal' and 'healthy' transition from childhood to adulthood.[12] As 'adolescents', young people were represented as a separate category of person, but precisely then to define them as dependent, in need of supervision and regulation. The status of the teenager consumer, on the other hand, as a separate category of person, was claimed to stem from the specificity and independent character of their needs, desires and interests.

In the early 1950s, the Australian print media frequently employed inverted commas around the term 'teenager'. 'Teenagers' appeared as consumer identities or in public representations of the leisure pursuits of 'charming' young women, but young people received little attention in these or in any other forms.[13] Over the next few years, this began to change, and as they achieved greater visibility, so too did the term 'teenager' appear more frequently and less problematically. Advertisers and media interests set out to create 'a world of their own' for teenagers by providing separate programmes, publications and consumer goods. The *Australian Women's Weekly* began publishing a teenage supplement in 1954, defining their interests as: love, fashion, people, parties, personal problems, discs – the latest recordings of popular stars – glamour tips and 'things to make' or sew. It promised to be a 'complete newspaper within a newspaper full of everything that matters when you're young and gay'.[14] 'Teenage' programmes on radio stations, with their 'teenage announcers', like Bert Newton and Ernie Sigley, set out to appeal to the general population of young people, as did the late Saturday afternoon shows which began to appear on commercial and Australian Broadcasting Commission (ABC) television at the end of the 1950s. Such strategies of creating a separate 'teenage world' strove to incite those very needs and desires these interests claimed to serve. While recognizing a potential new market, they were also busy attempting to create and foster one.

But their activities were not welcomed, by any means, by all members of society. Increasingly in the 1950s, a number of public figures expressed anxiety about the amount of media attention young people were receiving. John Medley, a prominent spokesperson on education, for instance, complained to a conference on 'Teenagers and their Problems' held by the Mental Hygiene Association of Australia in 1955 about too much attention being paid to young people. He warned against what he saw as a new tendency in contemporary society:

> At the moment the teenage stage is being treated in some quarters almost as if it were an end in itself. Papers publish special supplements devoted to their sartorial needs, Miss Teenage competitors achieve the full glare of publicity and teenage athletes are as much in the popular eye as their adult rivals.[15]

Such visibility, Medley suggested, could tempt the teenager to remain teenage and he urged a return to the 'old idea that adolescence is an awkward age which is best kept under cover as far as possible . . .'.[16]

Fig. 4 The teenage cabaret. A teenage dance being televised, Sydney 1960 (*Daily Telegraph*, 12 September, 1960).

In this statement, John Medley echoed the anxiety Franco Moretti claims has frequently been articulated since the nineteenth century through the figure of youth. Moretti describes the tensions which begin to emerge in the middle of that century around the threat consumer society was considered to pose to social and political order. It now seemed possible, he explains, for the individual to seek incessantly to 'put aside one's being and forge a new one'. As discussed in Chapter 3, Moretti analyses how these changes increas-ingly undermined the solution proposed by the BILDUNGSROMAN to reconcile 'the needs of the individual' with the 'needs of society'.[17] The promises of endless opportunities for individuals to transform their lives through having made a mockery of claims that youth – the period in one's life associated with experimentation and the making of a self – would necessarily come to an end. Similarly, then, John Medley in 1950s Australia lamented the dangers of 'tempting the teenager to remain teenage'. Modern society, he warned, defeated its own responsibility to itself and to young people to ensure that the period of youth should be circumscribed, supervised and eventually closed off.

In elaborating these concerns, Medley employed the term 'teenager' in a manner which was to have increasing currency in the late 1950s. In this context, the term spoke of a modern identity and claimed to identify a problem of a certain excessiveness among the young. Parents were called upon to monitor and supervise more carefully the leisure activities of their children – in particular, their reading of American comics.[18] Advice books and magazine and newspaper articles for parents promised to teach them about 'teenagers' and to offer guidance about how best to provide a 'stable' environment so that their children could make the 'difficult transition' from being a child to adult in the modern world.[19] But the term also served to domesticate or lessen any sense of threat that may have been posed by young people. The potential for excess, according to the type of claim made in these texts, arose from the 'normal' problems of living through the storm and stress of adolescence, aggravated by the conditions of modern life. The media may have been to blame in paying them too much attention, and in providing unwholesome fare, but the problem was considered a contained one.

The American comic strip 'Penny', which appeared both in the Melbourne newspaper, the *Age*, and in the *Sydney Morning Herald*, provides a vivid and amusing illustration of this mode of representing 'the teenager' in the 1950s and 1960s. Penny was portrayed as an exuberant young woman who often appeared, increasingly in the 1950s, to be manipulating the discourses of adolescence and popular psychology. She displayed little interest in school or boys, but was preoccupied with clothes, make-up, her hair, movies, popular music and talking on the telephone to her girlfriends. Framing the story of Penny, were her slightly frazzled but tolerant parents, and most often the solid figure of her father. Penny was depicted seeking countless ways to drag money out of her parents to cater for her endless desires for material goods. She asserted her need for a teenage life in the spaces of the parental home and in her leisure life. She

Fig. 5 The teenager body, all arms and legs. From the comic strip 'Penny' (*Sun-Herald*, 28 September 1958).

claimed to quote various authorities about teenagers in support of her understanding of her needs – such as the psychiatrist who recognized the importance of her desire to constantly play records while at home. But her father, and sometimes her mother, were always the knowing figures who mostly had the last word, even if only to themselves.[20] This comic strip depicted the home as the space of supervised freedom in which the teenager was allowed to express herself and indulge her teenagerhood under the gaze of her parents. The humour relied on a sense of recognition which claimed to acknowledge the necessity of youth to young people, just as it acknowledged the need for parents to be the benign – but nevertheless vigilant – superintendents of the teenager. Most clearly, however, the humour centred on the problems created for parents living with a figure which it represented as of a different species.

While the notion of the 'teenager' in the popular media tended to constitute the responsibilities of parents in benign terms and to domesticate the activities of young people, the category of the 'juvenile delinquent', however, presented these issues in a more threatening, more urgent form.

Troublesome youth

In the 1950s, the term 'juvenile delinquency' registered a set of concerns about the activities of young people and their supervision by institutions or individuals representing the social order. It spoke of the need for such regulation and the inadequacy of appropriate agencies in performing their tasks on behalf of the social and political order. But this apparent failure did not raise questions about the activities of these bodies nor the normative principles said to lie at the basis of their responsibilities. On the contrary, the rhetoric about juvenile delinquency in the media and in official reports served to underline and strengthen their claims to legitimacy.

Various state governments around Australia in the 1950s initiated formal inquiries into 'the problem of juvenile delinquency'.[21] In Victoria, to take one example, the publication of the report of the Barry Committee in July 1956 had been preceded by considerable media attention to this issue throughout 1954 and 1955.[22] Significantly, however, this committee had not instituted a public inquiry, but had proceeded to evaluate 'expert opinion' about the 'causes' of juvenile delinquency in order to pursue what it claimed to be a 'dispassionate approach' to the question of the nature and extent of juvenile delinquency in Victoria. Reviewing the evidence provided by psychologists, psychiatrists, sociologists, lawyers, judges and the police, the committee drew on both local and overseas professionals to develop its claim that juvenile delinquency could be clearly recognized as a social problem with identifiable social solutions. The committee concluded that the problem of juvenile delinquency was a problem of 'anti-social individuals . . . manufactured in childhood'.[23] Insecurity experienced early in life, it claimed, meant that the young person could not successfully make the transition through the difficult and turbulent emotional years of adolescence.

The family clearly emerged as the locus of the problem. The committee blamed a lack of cohesion found in the 'broken home' and 'where family life has suffered because, for example, both parents are working and the mother is not discharging the primary function of managing the home and caring for the children . . .'.[24] The committee claimed that 'the psychological conditions obtaining in the family' were more important than any other factor in causing the antisocial conduct of the juvenile delinquent.[25] In looking for 'methods of prevention', the Barry Committee recommended that the family be preserved and strengthened as a cohesive social unit. Central to this process, it claimed, was the return of all mothers to the domestic hearth, resuming their proper practice of the 'art of motherhood'. In this space of the family home, the child was to be adequately supervised – a task which required the delicate balancing of surveillance and discipline with the careful avoidance of being too 'overprotective'. The normal development of the adolescent required that parents provide the correct amounts of both security and freedom.[26]

Schools, churches, youth clubs, juvenile courts, child guidance experts, local councils and special policy units should surround the family unit, according to the Barry Committee, providing assistance and educative programmes for parents and their children. Overseeing all these agencies, the committee recommended, there should be a co-ordinating authority to ensure that all aspects of child welfare were provided for and to initiate research programmes to monitor and predict when and why delinquent behaviour might occur. These recommendations rested on an assumption of the necessity of an expanded role for an elaborate network of professionals and the institutions or organizations they represented. These agencies would map and monitor every aspect of the developing child's life. Young people's activities in the home, the classroom, the school playground, the street, the youth club and the milkbar all became legitimate spheres for the surveillance and activities of the 'expert'. Any signs of failure, disturbance or 'maladjustment' were to be addressed by educative interventions in the lives of both the children concerned and their parents.

This official literature identified adolescence as a particular stage of a young person's life, a stage when they were 'at risk' and in need of careful monitoring and attention. It constituted the adolescent as a separate category of person in much the same terms as did the educational and adolescent psychology literature, but proposed a much more elaborate vision of a disciplinary network or community alert to the needs and vulnerabilities of that identity. Media attention to juvenile delinquency similarly served to specify the features and characteristics of the adolescent, but its focus in terms of solutions tended to rest most often simply with the working mother and the neglect of her responsibilities.

In the Melbourne daily press during the year leading up to the publication of the Barry Committee's report, two figures dominated accounts of 'the problem of juvenile delinquency': American youth as represented in contemporary films and the Australian bodgie (and sometimes his female counterpart the widgie).[27] These were 'folk devils' in Stanley Cohen's terms.[28] They served to dramatize the problem and heighten the sense of threat to the social order in the context of the media's strategies to make headlines: 'Bodgies in Hold Up', 'Bodgie Widgie Gang Fights'.[29] The film 'The Blackboard Jungle', depicting life in a New York school, had been showing in the city's cinemas. 'Scenes reminiscent' of the film, the *Age* claimed in October that year, could now be seen in the streets of Melbourne.[30] At times, too, these two figures were combined: 'American influences' were blamed for the 'bodgie element' among Australian youth.

'The Blackboard Jungle' served not only to signify an image of potential danger – of what Australian youth could become – but also to indicate a growing recognition that the school could no longer be relied upon to provide proper supervision of young people. Newspaper reports in 1955 suggest that the school joined the street, the milkbar, the urban railway system and the unsupervised party as a potential space for 'troublesome youth' to demonstrate the inadequacy of parental supervision and discipline. A number of reports of 'children' and 'teenagers', 'too drunk to be taught', appeared suggesting that the school could not function as a place which rescued young people from the dangers of the street; they simply brought their habits of the street into the school. Other reports suggested that collecting young people together in such a setting as the school provided an environment which could breed rather than prevent juvenile delinquency.[31] But this inadequacy of the school only served to strengthen the claims of the 'experts' about the necessity of their intervention to determine appropriate norms and practices of training to be followed both by parents – the child's first teacher – and teachers.

Press reports and feature articles continued to promote these claims in subsequent years. Whether they were building up a sense of urgency about 'the juvenile delinquency problem' or playing it down, the statements of the broad range of professional groups now collecting around the figure of the adolescent played a major role. Criminologists, psychologists, social workers, youth workers, education researchers, statisticians and child welfare officers were readily quoted; the proliferation of these experts went unquestioned. So, too, did the inevitable conclusion of these reports about the need for greater surveillance of the family and home environment of young people. Some newspaper articles raised the question of whether parents themselves should be punished rather than the 'juvenile delinquents'. This possibility was always quickly rejected, but contemplating this apparently drastic action served once again to underline the apparent necessity of creating the right type of home environment – in which the correct combination of love and discipline would be provided – assisted and surrounded by the educative community and its associated forms of expertise.

Two very different studies on the 'bodgie' appeared in the second half of the 1950s. The first was an anthropological investigation undertaken by a student, John McDonald, at the University of Sydney. This study was picked up and became the subject of a newspaper report in 1956. The thesis described the history of bodgies in Sydney emerging in the years after the Second World War. Groups of young people took on the blue jeans, clothing and hairstyles of American seamen encountered during the war. McDonald argued that the young people of these groups were predominantly working class and that the adoption of this style was a response to the frustrations of being youth and working class in the Australia of the post-war era:

> Becoming a bodgie has provided a solution to the frustrating dilemma in which youths, particularly working class youths, are placed in our society. Becoming a bodgie has been easier than upward social mobility, while becoming a bodgie has been both easier, and faster, than becoming an adult.[32]

McDonald suggested that these young people had broken with many of the conventions of Australian life, including the dichotomy between the sexes and the sexual mores of that culture. He also stressed, however, that the bodgie groups he studied around Sydney were very diverse in cultural style and way of life.

The second study, *The Bodgie: A Study in Psychological Abnormality* (1958) by A.E. Manning, claimed to 'clarify the sociological and psychological problems facing a world with a substratum of troubled youth'. Unlike McDonald, Manning noted with dismay that traditional relations between the sexes were broken down in bodgie groups. Bodgies, he argued, were disturbed youth, hooligans, maladjusted. The emancipation of women and the education system was to blame in producing the widgie, the 'female counterpart' to this new form of hooligan, the bodgie:

> Women in their new freedom ceased to be educated as women. They seized upon the subject matter of male education and strove to equal or beat the male in his own field, without pausing to consider when or what form of education was desirable or valuable for their sex.[33]

Manning reported on 20 case studies of Australian and New Zealand bodgies and widgies. All were psychologically unbalanced in his terms, manifesting various types of emotional distress. They were children 'gone wrong' and society was at fault. The home, the church and the school had failed them, but the solution lay with these institutions too. Manning diagnosed a need for an educative community in similar terms to those used by the professionals discussed above in their analysis of the 'problem of juvenile delinquency'. But he focused his community more clearly around the child's mother: she should be the centre around whom the whole home should revolve. Everything depended on her attitude to the child. The expertise of teachers, psychologists and churchmen, he insisted, should be directed towards persuading 'unwilling parents to do their duty', not on making rules and laws.[34]

Sydney newspaper reviews of these two publications on the bodgie treated the topic light-heartedly. They indicated none of the anxiety which the Melbourne papers had demonstrated in the year leading up to the establishment of the Barry Committee. The Sydney reports treated the bodgie story as primarily a fashion item, a tale of changing fads among young people. The account of the scholarly university study was juxtaposed with an article quoting a Sydney hairdresser who claimed that the bodgie look was now fashionable with all young men, whereas the widgie look was 'out': young women, it declared, were now all converting to the Audrey Hepburn look.[35] Similarly, a newspaper review of the Manning book made light of his concerns. Its headline, 'Treating the bodgie much too seriously', echoed John Medley's complaint about paying too much attention to young people. Elevating 'these ridiculous young people' to the status of a 'social problem', the article suggested, would simply provide these 'posturing teenagers' with the 'great kick' they were looking for.[36]

Fig. 6 The bodgies: Teenagers queueing to see the film 'Rock Around the Clock', Sydney 1956. The article describes some of the crowd as 'bodgies' and wearing 'bizarre pink and black coats, pink shirts and ties. Others sported green suits and sovepipe [*sic*] trousers' (*Daily Telegraph*, 16 September 1956).

These reports on the bodgie, both in their original context and in the newspaper articles, included young women – the widgies – in their discussion of the activities of these groups of young people. As a symbol of 'troublesome youth', this distinguished them from 'juvenile delinquents' who were predominantly represented as male. Bodgies and widgies were troublesome because their presence as gangs on the street indicated a group of young people beyond or rejecting the supervisory care of adult and professional figures. Their interest in things American indicated their supposed gullibility, their vulnerability to manipulation, and hence served to underline, according to the Manning report, why this supervision of young people was necessary. The gendering of juvenile delinquency, on the other hand, suggested that it was young men who were more susceptible to the problems of being an adolescent in the modern world. They were the ones who, in the absence of the correct combination of supervision, freedom and love, would be most likely to break out, go 'out of control', as the 'natural' male aggressive instincts rose to the surface.

In the years leading up to the establishment of the Barry Committee in Victoria, the press reports of 'juvenile delinquency' had certainly represented it as predominantly a gendered problem in these terms. Where young women were mentioned, their misdemeanours were deemed to indicate that they were in need of care and the protection of the state.[37] Their actions were defined as those of a child; the activities of young men, on the other hand, were represented as revealing a more specific problem of adolescence. The committee continued this definition of the problem. They drew on the book *The Young Delinquent* by the English psychologist, Cyril Burt, who in turn had accepted G. Stanley Hall's view that adolescence should be understood as masculine and delinquent. According to Hall, every young man was a potential delinquent as he negotiated this difficult period of his life. But young women, he claimed, simply remained children and hence in need of protection. Hall declared women too emotionally and physically weak to be able or allowed to make the journey of adolescence.[38] Though the Barry committee included young women in its definition of the delinquent – males and females under the age of 17 convicted by the Children's Court of Victoria or engaging in conduct which could lead to conviction – much of its discussion and recommendations continued to work within this assumption of the gendered character of the problem. For instance, their recommendations, about the importance of expanding the work of youth clubs in Victoria defined the problem, as Bannister points out, as predominantly one of the lack of properly supervised leisure spaces for young males.[39]

This gendering of juvenile delinquency cut across the apparent neutrality of the statements about adolescence circulating in and around the space of the modern secondary school. The public discourses about juvenile delinquency represented all young people as in need of the assistance of proper adult care; but for young women this most often meant protection – their retention in the world of childhood dependency. Young men, on the other hand, needed that delicate combination of freedom and supervision said to be necessary to adolescence which would allow them to make the transition to independent adulthood. Though it might be 'masculine biologies' – the 'natural' male 'aggression instinct' – which caused potential problems in their making this transition, it was also somehow masculinity which enabled them to be adolescent and to take on the tasks of becoming a modern individual. The democratizing of the secondary school had been accompanied by a universalizing of the norms of adolescence to constitute a general category of young people. But in the realm of law-and-order discourses which set out to differentiate – to create a means of distinguishing between sections of the population – in order to effect more efficient means of surveillance and regulation of the population as a whole, these norms were utilized in the processes of marking off and identifying those said to be most in need of particular programmes of social administration. Youth as a separate category of person in this context was predominantly a gendered one with young women being relegated to the world of the child.

Some reports did appear, however, about the troublesome behaviour of young women. The assumptions about the gendered nature of the capacity of young people to engage in criminal and delinquent behaviour must surely have been threatened by the case of two New Zealand girls. Their trial received considerable press coverage in Australia in 1954. These accounts represented the case as revolving around the question of whether the girls were certifiable – abnormal or normal. They had been charged with the murder of one of their mothers; their defence counsellor was claiming 'paranoia of an exalted type and folie à deux communicated insanity'.[40] Headlines like 'Teenagers on Trial called "Dirty-minded"' and 'Teenage Murderers Showed No Regret' suggested this abnormality, yet at the same time the reference to 'teenagers' appeared to link this case to the more everyday reports of youthful crime and misdemeanours which were 'normally' those of young men.

Psychological experts were brought in to testify as to their insanity. Their sexuality was questioned with references to their 'wild infatuation' with each other. The nature of the crime itself was claimed to be sufficient to point to just how insane they were. And their lack of interest in the royal tour by the Queen received a mention as a clear indication that they were not 'normal' teenagers.[41] These psychological explanations contained the threatening nature of the crime: abnormal sexuality and insanity set the girls apart from society and hence unable to challenge conventional notions of 'what girls are capable of'. But at the same time, the very terms in which the case was reported suggested disturbing links with the normal – 'modern teenagers' and their tendency to excess – as did the reported comments of the Crown Prosecutor. He declared them 'incurably bad', rather than incurably insane. He argued that the girls had known what they were doing and that it was wrong in the 'eyes of the law and the community'. This, he said, was 'a cold, callously planned and premeditated murder, committed by two highly intelligent but precocious and dirty-minded little girls'.[42] This language suggested the potential dangers that lurked behind that excessiveness of the modern teenager allowed to live too much in a world of his or her own.[43] Young people were to be recognized as a separate category of person – a group to be differentiated from both children and adults – but they were not to live in a world of their own. They needed, according to such reports, to live in a world carefully supervised and monitored by appropriate adult forms of authority. The newspaper accounts of this trial served to dramatize the consequences of the absence of such regulation.

Reporting the problems of juvenile delinquency in feminine form often served to highlight the urgency of the need for programmes of social administration which treated young people as a separate category of person. For instance, in 1952, the committal by the Children's Court of a 16-year-old girl to Pentridge Gaol in Melbourne was described as 'a barbaric relic of medieval times' by the Deputy Leader of the Opposition.[44] Two girls, it appeared, had been incarcerated at Pentridge. Politicians were joined by local and visiting professional experts in the field of children's welfare in protesting about the lack of adequate provisions for juvenile delinquents as a general category of youthful offenders, and a number of letters to the editor appeared in Melbourne newspapers on the topic. The *Age* berated the State of Victoria as 'a neglectful parent' and called on the Child Welfare Department to establish institutions which could provide the proper treatment and education for all young people in its care.[45]

Similarly, in 1960, reports of young women of 13 and 14 years of age being used as prostitutes in 'expresso bars' provoked calls for increased policing of 'the suburbs' and for greater parental vigilance in monitoring the activity of young people.[46] The Victorian government had just brought in a new Social Welfare Act and its official spokespersons pointed to the provisions recommended in that Act as able to deal with such problems. It would ensure, the Chief Secretary claimed, that there was an expansion of social welfare institutions and staff trained specifically in the treatment and supervision of young people; new directors of family welfare and youth welfare, new family advisory and counselling services, new training centres and homes for young people, and a new research and statistics division.[47] Just as the Barry Committee had recommended, a new disciplinary community was to be set up combining the functions of education, surveillance and monitoring organized around the figure of the young person 'at risk', and focusing on the need to intervene in their lives and the lives of their families. The innocent body of the young adolescent girl in this instance became a powerful symbol of 'youth at risk' and a warning of the need for urgent government action. Modern times were blamed for the extent of freedom parents now gave to their daughters;[48] the supervision which should be provided in the space of the home would now have to be extended to penetrate every space of the modern city.

Another solution existed, however, as newspaper editorials at times pointed out. In such contexts, the image of organized youth was counterpoised with that of the troublesome, delinquent youth. The former, as I will indicate in the following section, was based on a particular notion of what a modern citizenry should look like, which began to lose its legitimacy in the 1960s. But in the previous decade, this form of youth-on-the-streets (and, more generally, the activities of young people in organized youth clubs) was reported in admiring terms by the press and government documents as the guise which all young people should adopt and an obvious solution in dealing with 'youth at risk'.

Organized youth

An *Age* editorial in 1958 announced the annual event of what was now referred to as the 'British Commonwealth Youth Sunday' march (previously known as the 'Empire Youth Sunday' march) as providing an effective counter to 'juvenile depravity'. These occasions, the editorial declared, should challenge young people to 'effective living and humanitarian service'. But it also commended them as assuring young people 'that they have a place peculiarly their own in the general scheme of things'.[49] This emphasis on giving young people a sense of their place, of their social importance – 'peculiarly their own' – marked a significant shift from the claims made for this event at the beginning of the decade. Some seven years earlier, the same newspaper, using the rhetoric of faith, honour and shame, welcomed the 'Empire Youth Sunday' as providing the moment when youth could demonstrate their preparedness for citizenship. Young people, according to this editorial, should be urged to 'take life seriously, and shoulder its heaviest responsibilities, for their own sakes'.[50] In 1951, youth had remained primarily a traditional figure, already taking on the characteristics of the convinced citizen, and indeed, in these marches, providing a useful image of what that figure was about. In 1958, on the other hand, the same event was welcomed as a means of publicly recognizing youth as a separate category of person.

These events had begun in England in 1937 with the coronation of King George VI. Other modes of creating groups of organized youth had an even longer history. The Young Men's Christian

On Parade in the Empire Youth March

● TWELVE THOU-SAND SCHOOL CHILDREN in the Empire Youth March approach down Swanston Street yesterday on their way to city churches. Eyes turn right at the Town Hall, where the Governor (Sir Dallas Brooks) takes the salute. Later, he went to the service in St. Paul's Cathedral.

Fig. 7 Organized youth: 'Citizens-in-the-making' on an Empire Youth March, Melbourne (*Age*, 7 May 1956).

Association (YMCA), the Young Women's Christian Association (YWCA), the Boy Scouts Association and Girl Guides, had all begun in the nineteenth century or early in the twentieth century, and again drew on or were directly connected with British organizations.[51] The Commonwealth Government began to take an interest in co-ordinating the work of these youth organizations in the years after the Second World War, as did the various state governments. Co-ordinating committees in each state were established, mostly concerned with programmes of physical fitness for young people.

A 1952 report prepared for the newly established Commonwealth Office of Education attempted to document the full range of government-sponsored and voluntary youth organizations existing in every state of Australia at the beginning of the 1950s. This report noted two major shifts occurring at this point in time to the ways in which these bodies were attempting to organize youth. First, it noted, those associations which had in the past sought to provide activities and forms of organization for a general category of children had now begun to create two separate bodies – one for 'children' and one for 'youth'. Church organizations were setting up junior and senior groups as was the Boy Scouts Association, which had recently established a Senior Scouts group for 15–17½-year-olds. The distinctive feature of these separate organizations for 'youth' appeared to be that their programmes were based on notions of cooperation rather than obedience to authority, thereby catering, the author of the report suggested, for the 'desire of adolescents for self-expression and independence'.[52] Youth were thereby being recognized and defined in these contexts as a separate category of person with distinctive needs and characteristics.

Second, this report noted the expanding role of professional youth leaders and welfare workers in these youth organizations. Voluntary and government-sponsored agencies had shifted from using amateur youth workers to, at first, trained volunteers, and now to the increasing employment of professionally trained youth leaders. The professional status of these latter workers was limited (a fact reflected in their conditions of work and levels of remuneration); but they had become crucial to the survival of these agencies. The report called for greater co-ordination in the training of youth workers and, more generally, the activities of the agencies themselves. It proposed that the Departments of Education in each state set up separate sections for youth education with Superintendents of Youth Education responsible for co-ordinating educational programmes for youth and it recommended the establishment of State Youth Councils to co-ordinate government and voluntary organizations concerned with education and leisure programmes for youth.[53] The latter proposal was eventually taken up by state governments, but more in connection with local imperatives than as a response to this report. In Victoria, for instance, the Youth Organizations Assistance Act was passed in 1957, after the publication of the report of the Barry Committee, and established a Youth Organizations Assistance Committee, which was later renamed the Youth Advisory Council after the passing of the Social Welfare Act in 1960.[54]

Youth clubs for boys rather than girls were seen as more urgent in the surveillance and regulation of young people. The New South Wales Police Commissioner, for instance, was reported in 1957 as saying that 'he did not think parents had as much difficulty in keeping their daughters off the streets and out of trouble as they did with sons'.[55] Clubs for young women had often begun as an offshoot of organizations established for boys only. The Girl Guides was the most famous of these, but the pattern prevailed in more local organizations such as the Victorian Association of Youth Clubs which had changed its name in 1953 from 'Boys' to 'Youth' in recognition of the growing numbers of girls already members of their local groups. Reports (in the daily press) of the activities of young women in youth clubs suggested that they were provided with programmes clearly differentiated according to notions of gender-appropriate projects. Cooking, sewing, physical culture, ballet, craftwork, and personal grooming, social etiquette and deportment classes were frequently mentioned alongside athletic and basketball competitions.

These forms of organized youth were seen as an effective antidote to problems of troublesome youth on the street. In the late 1950s, however, they began to be proposed by some commentators as a way of containing a set of youthful activities which had begun to gain popularity in other spaces. A number of church spokesmen suggested that the sponsorship of dances by youth clubs was one way to regulate and control the new craze among young people for rock 'n' roll music.[56] A newspaper article in 1959, for instance, provided an account of 'teenagers' praying while resting after 'dancing to the rock-'n'-roll beat' at a Methodist church hall in Melbourne.[57] But for the most part, newspaper stories about teenagers and rock 'n' roll reported young people as beyond the reach of formal adult authority or understanding.

Yet, the teenage fan and the teenage dancer were forms of 'youth-on-the-street' towards whom the daily newspapers appeared to have a relatively benign or, at least, ambivalent attitude in the 1950s. Though young people in these guises were apparently beyond the control of legitimate forms of adult authority, they were not clearly condemned or judged by the press. The action of the Parramatta local council in banning the Australian popular singing star, Johnny O'Keefe, from playing his rock 'n' roll music in their local halls in 1958, for instance, was reported from O'Keefe's point of view. The headlines to the article quoted him as saying the 'Mayor is a Square' and it went on to report his reactions to the council's ban.[58] Similarly, the antics of young people at rock 'n' roll concerts or in welcoming the latest American singer arriving at the airport received none of the disapproval that was expressed so often about 'bodgies' and 'widgies'. 'Bad' young people, it appeared, became juvenile delinquents; 'good' young people merely became the misguided but harmless 'teenage fans'.

The 'teenage fan' was a relatively new phenomenon. Johnny Ray, America's 'crying crooner', for instance, was reported in 1953 as attracting a female audience 'from middle-aged down to moppets in jeans and bobby-sox'.[59] The 'teenage fan', which was still largely a female phenomenon but now also differentiated by age, became a more recognizable figure in 1954 when the Australian entrepreneur,

Lee Gordon, who had arranged Johnny Ray's tour, began to bring
out an ever-increasing number of American stars. Bill Haley, who
claimed to have invented rock 'n' roll, performed at the Sydney
stadium in two shows at the beginning of 1957 to an audience
of 22,000 young people. His film, 'Rock around the Clock', had
been said to cause 'frenzied teenagers' in America and England
to 'sway, stamp, rip cinema seats, fling fire-crackers, break bottles
and block traffic'.[60] These newspaper stories no doubt served as a
useful marketing strategy for the film and for his visit to Australia.
But no hysterical scenes were reported as occurring here. The audiences at the stadium danced in the aisles, but caused no major
disruptions and certainly no trouble. Even the crowd scenes of
weeping and screaming women reported as occurring when Johnny
Ray arrived at Sydney airport from the USA or of 4,000 teenage fans
at Essenden airport when Fabian flew to Melbourne from Sydney
did not appear to cause any serious problems for the police or other
officials.[61]

But in 1964, the Beatles were greeted by crowds of unprecedented
size of adoring fans – mostly teenage girls. Twenty thousand fans
were reported to have jammed the streets of Melbourne.[62] Discussing
the welcome received by this group from their teenage fans on their
first visit to America earlier in that same year, Barbara Ehrenreich *et
al.* argue that this was the first mass outburst of the 1960s to feature
women. It was, they suggest, 'the first and most dramatic uprising
of *women's* sexual revolution':

> To abandon control – to scream, faint, dash about in mobs –
> was, in form if not in conscious intent, to protest the sexual
> repressiveness, the rigid double standard of female teen cul-
> ture.[63]

As teen fans, these authors suggest, young women became active
sexually – they were laying claim to sexual feelings and constituting
themselves as the pursuers, rather than simply objects of the desir-
ing male gaze.[64]

Ehrenreich *et al.* point to the eagerness of social commentators
in America, and psychologists in particular, to explain the phenomenon of 'Beatlemania'. David Riesman described it as 'a form of
protest against the adult world', whereas at least one psychologist
looked to explain it away as simply the behaviour of young women
going through the normal stresses and strains of the emotional and
physical growth associated with adolescence.[65] In Australia, too,
psychological explanations of Beatlemania predominated. Perhaps
one of the most interesting set of comments reported in the press
was that of a Melbourne professor, A.R. Chisholm, who described

Beatlemania as a frantic attempt by teenagers to rediscover their 'lost homeland' of 'uninhibited youthfulness'. But, he declared,

> this 'emancipation' from the dreariness of an overstandardised world is itself a form of standardisation, and this defeats its own ends. Joshua blows his trumpets to knock down the cramping walls, and trumpet-blowing becomes a mass-production process.[66]

The scenes of Beatlemania in Australia – of youth-on-the-streets – reported and pictured on the front page of the daily newspapers, presented young people in a quite different guise to the images of youth taking part in the Empire Youth Sunday marches in previous years. The Melbourne *Age* front page report with its headline, '50 Teenagers hurt in Wild City Crush: Beatles' Welcoming Crowd Jams Streets', concentrated on the fans hurt in the crush and the comments of police who were reported making fairly benign remarks about the whole event. Young people in these 1964 scenes were not the orderly citizens-in-the-making of the youth marches; they were out of control. They were attracting considerable attention and asserting a very distinctive presence for themselves – as 'teenagers' – but they were also depicted as 'teenagers' in media accounts, and as non-threatening in this form. Significantly, the Commonwealth Youth Sunday march through the streets of Melbourne was cancelled in 1965, because, according to the report in the *Age*, 'some of the children, particularly the boys, thought a march old-fashioned'.[67]

In the same year, another form of youthful presence on the street was gaining momentum: the student protester. While the teenage fan, seen in such large numbers in the mid-1960s, was a figure which had emerged in the 1950s, the history of the student protester was marked by some significant shifts in this period. Students had appeared on the streets in the 1950s, but their presence during this decade was largely in the form of a group of young people being 'children' for a day. University commemoration day parades – young people having fun, making a nuisance of themselves – received some media attention, but their activities were reported in these terms with no connections being made to youth as a modern separate category of person. Even a student protest in the streets of Sydney in 1956 against public transport fare rises was conducted and reported in the press in the form of such a commemoration day 'prank'.[68] In this case, as it seemed in all other instances, the student appeared to be predominantly a masculine figure.

In 1956, students took to the streets of Melbourne, however, to demonstrate their concern about international political events:

Fig. 8 The teenage fan: Beatlemania. Crowds of teenagers took over the streets of Melbourne in 1964 when the Beatles first visited Australia (*Age*, 15 June 1964).

(a)

Fig. 9 (a) The student protester in the 1950s. Students from Sydney University protesting against fare rises in a Commemoration Day, 'youthful prank' style (*Sydney Morning Herald*, 3 July 1956). (b) The student protester in the 1960s. By 1964, students had become 'troublesome youth' as they took to the streets to protest about international and national political issues (*Sydney Morning Herald*, 7 May 1964).

Britain's sending of troops into Suez and the USSR's invasion of Hungary.[69] This was a forerunner of a form of student politics and public demonstration which they would begin to take up with some frequency in the next decade; but it was not until the 1960s that their actions began to be treated by public spokespersons as 'a problem of modern youth'. Public officials and the media now began to

UNIVERSITY ACTION ON "GRAVE" CHARGES ON STUDENTS

The Vice-Chancellor of Sydney University, Professor S. H. Roberts, said last night that accusations about student behaviour on Commemoration Day yesterday were "particularly grave."

He said they were so grave they could quickly bring the university into disrepute.

Professor Roberts said that if a police report showed students were responsible for the disturbances, the Students' Representative Council, himself or the university's Proctorial Board could take disciplinary action against the students concerned.

In Commemoration Day clashes between students and police, 38 men, women and youths were arrested and charged—34 after a wild melee outside the U.S. Consulate in Bligh Street.

Four students were arrested in Hyde Park. One of them was swimming in the Archibald Fountain.

Early yesterday morning, underwear was hung on the Cenotaph in Martin Place. Students were suspected of the desecration.

The Acting Commissioner of Police, Mr S. Windsor, last night said serious consideration would have to be given to whether any more university Commemoration Day processions should be allowed.

POLICE STOP DEMONSTRATION

Police battling to control a crowd of Sydney University students during the demonstration in Wynyard Street yesterday.

(b)

use the rhetoric which had developed around the figure of the juvenile delinquent to define and contain the threat of the activities of these young people. In 1960, students again appeared on the streets – and in the daily newspapers – as protesters; this time, they were expressing their anger about the massacre at Sharpeville in South Africa. In the 1956 demonstration, students had simply been diverted by police down the back streets of Melbourne; in 1960, the daily press reported 'police clash with students'. Ten people were arrested in the Sydney demonstration against South Africa and police were reported to have 'repeatedly charged about 1,000 chanting students'. The magistrate hearing the case against students arrested during this demonstration was reported to have told them that the events in South Africa 'were a matter only for the Commonwealth Government'.[70] Another magistrate at a later hearing similarly told students they should 'mind their own business' and leave 'international affairs to people who know something about them'.[71] In the form of Empire or Commonwealth Youth Sunday marches, it was legitimate for young people to consider themselves citizens-in-the-making with a responsibility to be concerned with what was happening in the world around them. As youth-on-the-streets beyond adult control, they were placed in the category of 'modern youth' and 'adult authority' reasserted its regulatory powers to silence the voices of this new category of persons it had sought, in other contexts, to create.

Issues of race and racism figured as a central focus of these
forms of student protest over the next few years. In 1961, students
demonstrated against Australia's 'White Australia Policy' at a number
of election meetings in Melbourne[72] and, in 1965, students gained
considerable attention in their protests against racism towards
Aboriginal people in the country towns of New South Wales. In this
latter instance, the *Sydney Morning Herald*, in two major editorials,
came out in support of the students who had undertaken a bus tour
of a number of these towns, drawing attention to racial discrimina-
tion practices. The 'students' mission is commendable evidence', it
said, that '35 young Australians care sufficiently about the future of
aborigines to forsake Sydney's tempting summer beaches . . .'.[73]

The street demonstrations against the Menzies government's con-
scription legislation and Australia's involvement in the Vietnam War
which began to gain momentum that same year were recognized as
bringing together a broader section of the population than simply
students. Media reports of these events, however, provide useful
evidence that the student, and the student protester in particular,
continued to be understood as a masculine figure. In October 1965,
for instance, 400 people were reported to have 'clashed violently
with police' in a 'sit-down demonstration against the Vietnam war';
the newspaper story described the demonstration as made up of
'students, unionists and some women'.[74] The gendered assumptions
about the student protester were strengthened by the connections
drawn between this figure and that of the beatnik and of the 'angry
young man' of the late 1950s and early 1960s. Media reports on
these latter two figures represented them as predominantly overseas
phenomena and as characteristically masculine.[75] The protests of
Australian students were acknowledged by these reports as part
of an international movement of young people, but they were also
contained by their representation in this form as simply another
manifestation of a certain excessiveness to be found among youth
in the modern world.

Youth appeared 'on the street' in many guises in the 1950s and
early 1960s. Public discussion of this youthful public presence –
troublesome or otherwise – depicted youth as predominantly masculine. The modern category of youth deployed in these instances
defined a social group in need of both supervision and freedom. The
delicate balance required between these two needs, it was claimed,
created a group 'at risk', who must be surrounded by a range of
institutions and professional groups charged with the responsibility
of ensuring that young people grow up in the appropriate social
environment. The presence of the 'teenage fan' and the 'student
protester' on the streets, however, demonstrated the instability

of this category of youth. The marketing of commodities specifically for a teenage market spoke to young women, in particular, as having distinctive needs and desires of their own. In this context, they were more than simply 'children' or 'women' – they were a separate category of person. On the streets, as 'the teenage fan', they adopted this public identification with gay abandon. They proclaimed themselves 'members of the public' with a set of pleasures and preoccupations very much part of a world of their own. As 'student protesters', on the other hand, young people took seriously the claim made in the context of education and organized youth activities that they were 'citizens-in-the-making'. They asserted a voice for themselves 'as youth' and demanded to be heard on matters of local and international significance.

7 /// 'The best of everything': defining the space of the teenage girl

The 'best of everything' for young women in the 1950s, according to the novel and the film of this title, was love. The central female characters worked in a modern, streamlined office, located in a shiny New York skyscraper. Each strove to be successful in her career, but it was the need for love that they all really shared. Joan Crawford starred in the film as the woman who misses out.[1] Released in 1959, the film explored a theme frequently taken up in the American cinema of the 1940s and 1950s which described a tension in women's lives between their involvement in the sphere of production and their reproductive role – a contradiction between the category 'worker' and 'women'.[2] But the film did portray young women successfully participating in the modern world of work and thriving in the environments of the modern office and the modern city: modernity provided them access to the 'best of everything', as long as they did not lose sight of the most important of their needs – to be 'the loved individual' of the classic romance narrative.[3]

This chapter examines the emergence of the image of the teenage girl in the 1950s and early 1960s. Through the definition of this particular social subject, the consumer industries set out to create a form of agency committed to a project of subjective fulfilment through narcissistic consumption. Central to their campaign was the message that young women were the particular beneficiaries of modernity. In seeking to constitute the relationship between young women and modernization in these terms, these industries set out to incite in this social group a personal investment in those processes – as well as in the position of consumer – as being central to what their lives were about. This chapter begins by extending the discussion, begun in Chapter 4, about the way women's relationship to modernity was represented in the Australian print media in this period. It then turns to examine the more specific ways in which young women were being told they should understand themselves as 'modern girls'. In this first section, too, I look at how the image of the teenage girl conjured up by the consumer industries sought to define young women as first and foremost sexed identities. The second section discusses the tensions and difficulties which these representations of female subjectivity reveal and I explore further how popular representations of young women sought to shape the way young women understood their growing up and girlhood. Finally, I discuss the possibilities and problems which this defining of the social space of the teenage girl opened up for young women in this period and, in particular, the way popular discourses about her growing up represented this period in her life as a circumscribed one, as a time which must come to an appropriate end (in marriage, of course).

'What interests teenage girls?'

By 1964, when a feature article in Sydney's *Sun-Herald* asked the question 'What interests teenage girls?', a great deal of advertising time and money had already gone into ensuring that local Australian industries could predict the answer. The article reported the findings of a study, titled 'Girls at Leisure', conducted in Britain by a group of youth organizations. Playing down the extent to which the young women studied differed from their mothers or even grandmothers, this newspaper report claimed that 'Much of what makes girls "difficult" . . . is . . . that sense of being crammed into a mould labelled "woman" when what the adolescent really wants is to be recognised as the complex individual she really is.'[4] It is significant that this statement acknowledged the complexity of the ways in which young women understand who they are and what their lives are about. But its argument that no difference existed between generations of women ignored the extent to which the young women of whom it spoke were subject to new influences and pressures. The fashion industry and associated interests of the 1950s sought precisely to 'cram' young women into 'the mould labelled "woman"', to persuade young women to think of themselves as 'women' and to do so in very particular ways. They set out to ensure that young women devoted their lives to a pattern of consumption concerned with their own self-image, both in terms of their personal appearance as well as with the look of things around them in the spaces they occupied. In these terms, the experiences of growing up and girlhood for young women in this period were being shaped in quite different ways to those of previous generations of women. This chapter looks at these processes.

A number of writers have commented on the major transformations in everyday life which occurred in advanced Western industrial societies in the years after the Second World War. Some speak of the 1950s, others of the period from 1945 until the early 1960s, as marking the period of change. Henri Lefebvre, for instance, describes social planners after the Second World War as 'exploiting consumption as a means of organising everyday life'. He argues that the development of satellite suburbs and urban developments in this period programmed people's lives, laying out their daily lives like pieces in a puzzle. In the tradition of the modernist cultural critics discussed in Chapter 2, Lefebvre depicts women as the victims of these processes of modernization. Everyday life, he claims, 'weighs heaviest on women':

> Some are bogged down by its peculiar cloying substance, others escape into make believe . . . they have their own substitutes; they complain – about men, the human condition, life, God and the gods – but they are always beside the point; they are the subjects of everyday life and its victims or objects and substitutes (beauty, femininity, fashion, etc.) and it is at their cost that substitutes thrive. Likewise they are both buyers and consumers of commodities and symbols for commodities (in advertisements, nudes and smiles).[5]

It was precisely the force of these changes in reorganizing women's lives, Mica Nava argues, to which Betty Friedan was responding in writing of the 'feminist mystique'.[6] Friedan, like Lefebvre, represents women as the victims of these processes of modernization. Frederic Jameson, on the other hand, simply notes the emergence of a new kind of society after the war, characterized by such changes as the appearance of new types of consumption and the 'penetration of advertising, television and the media generally to a hitherto unparalleled degree throughout society'.[7] It is clear that modern forms of lifestyle advertising addressing a female consumer emerged before the Second World War;[8] the distinctiveness of the 1950s and early 1960s lies, however, in the extent to which this advertising, and the patterns of consumption it sought to promote, permeated and organized the everyday life of vast sections of the population. It is also clear that women were at the forefront of these developments. This chapter explores the complexity of their relationship to these processes of modernization in Australia in the 1950s and early 1960s and, in particular, the contradictory nature of the changes which transformed the lives of young women in this period.

Popular representations of these changes in the Australian print media and publicity material of the period constituted women as the beneficiaries of modernity. Women were to live in a 'stream-lined push-button' future of modern laundries, modern kitchens, dream homes and 'self-contained suburbs' served by the new 'drive-in' shopping centres and theatres.[9] In these images, modern science appeared as benign, domestic; it served everyday life rather than transforming it. 'Science will come increasingly into the home', said one newspaper article, 'to lighten household chores in scores of new ways and make life brighter, easier and more gracious . . .'.[10] Modern science served the everyday-feminine, too, in publicity material pro-claiming that it provided the materials through which women could transform not only their bodies but their personalities. This rhetoric celebrated modern science and the modern consumer society as creating, in Laura Mulvey's terms, a 'democracy of glamour'. Adver-tising, the packaging and display of products and the movies of this period promoted the image that all women could and should par-ticipate in this world of glamour, this world of creating desirable appearances. The 1950s, says Mulvey, 'completed a process, through movies and through mass-produced clothes and cosmetics, that had been launched in the thirties and interrupted by the Second World War'.[11]

Advertising campaigns by the clothing and cosmetics industries in Australia targeted young women increasingly in these same terms in the 1950s as a separate sector of the female market. At the be-ginning of the decade, advertisements or feature articles specifically addressed to young women were likely to use labels like 'the modern miss', 'business girls' or 'juniors', but articles about 'making your own clothes' indicated that mass-produced clothes remained beyond the budgets of many young women.[12] The appearance of the special column in the *Australian Women's Weekly*, which began in 1954 and became a separate section as *The Teenagers' Weekly* in 1959, how-ever, signalled that this market was becoming well-established as having distinctive needs and interests by the middle of the 1950s. Other magazines also appeared for the teenage girl in the last few years of this decade, though most were short-lived.[13] Daily news-papers similarly carried advertisements and feature articles addressed to 'the teenage girl' and department stores set up separate sections with names like the 'Hi-Teen Department', the 'Young Sydney Shop' and 'The Younger Set Girl', decorated with modern furniture and painted in the latest modern shades.[14] 'The teenage girl' was now a clearly delineated figure in these contexts, consumed with her ap-pearance and keen to be clothed in the latest fashions.

Publicity campaigns and advertising directed at 'young women' as a specific category purported to speak of their desires.[15] Paramount in this world of needs and longings, according to these campaigns, was the young woman's wish to look feminine at all times, even though the nature of that look changed dramatically during the course of the decade. At the beginning of the 1950s, a demure 'girlishness' of 'fresh' cotton dresses defined the fashion industry's image of 'feminine loveliness'; in the mid- to late 1950s, an elegant, glamorous femininity required Paris 'chic' fashions and the shortening of the skirt; by the early 1960s, a 'modern youthfulness' was emphasized and the 'Jackie Kennedy' look was 'in' with 'neat' jackets, schoolgirl-style 'breton' hats and short skirts. The cosmetic and beauty market boomed with similarly changing fashions promoted as essential to the young woman's retaining her claim to true 'feminine loveliness'.[16] Articles appeared in the print media instructing young women on how much make-up to wear as well as the appropriate style for the latest fashions. And the foundation garment industry set out to appeal to young women with feature articles about how they now designed underwear especially for the young woman 'because you're "all woman"'.[17] These industries were working hard to mobilize the desires of young women to be concerned with their appearances, with how they looked.[18] They set out to augment their needs and aspirations and to persuade them that these could be satisfied by the purchasing of the latest fashions made especially for 'the teenage girl'.

While the shift from images of 'girlishness' to 'modern youthful femininity' in representations of teenage girls during the decade points to the eagerness of the fashion industries to foster new markets with distinct needs and desires, it also indicates the force of other influences shaping female subjectivities, particularly by the late 1950s. The emphasis on youth or the adolescent as a separate category of person in other contexts meant that representations of young women as thoroughly consumed with presenting their bodies in appropriate feminine form had to be adapted to recognize these changes. The appearance of 'the sack' drew a great deal of comment in 1958 as beauty and fashion consultants contemplated whether its straight, shapeless lines made a mockery of the notions of the 'womanly shape' they had devoted their lives to. They condemned the sack as 'unfeminine', 'boyish', 'unglamorous' and claimed young women looked 'all-arms-and-legs'.[19] But this look gained the approval of some key figures in the world of glamour: Marilyn Monroe was quoted as 'liking the sack look'[20] and Princess Margaret was photographed wearing the latest bright coloured stockings which emphasized this same leggy look.[21]

These clothing styles encouraged a teenage femininity which departed considerably from the images of girlish, demure femininity prominent at the beginning of the decade. But it was the apparent tendency of some teenage girls to disregard fashion completely, or rather to pursue their own notions of modes of dress appropriate to their age, which caused the most consternation. Newspaper reports of girls in 'battered jeans' and 'duffle coats' appeared – not only in the fashion sections but in other parts of such publications – discussing whether the adoption of such styles of dress intimated a future of delinquency.[22] Though they concluded that this behaviour did not have such serious implications, these articles discussed the 'antics' of such young women in terms which echoed the way the category of 'the teenager' was employed in other contexts to signal a certain excessiveness among modern youth and the need for parental vigilance.[23]

The apparent disregard of feminine fashions by at least some young women and the increasing importance of fashions which emphasized 'youthful' shapes and colours indicated that the teenage girl was increasingly taking on her own shape in the late 1950s. She was no longer demure femininity waiting patiently for her mature womanhood to begin; she was enjoying her youth, her teenagerhood. By the early 1960s, 'teenage girl' fashions dominated the images being sold by the clothing and cosmetics industries to young women: the 'mod' look, specifically geared to a 'modern youthful' market, was 'in'.[24] Thus these industries addressed young women as 'women' who, as such, would want to present their bodies and selves as 'all woman'; but they also increasingly, in this period, began to recognize and shape this market as representing a separate group with their own distinct needs and interests. Publicity material and fashion feature articles in the print media now urged young women to resist the desire to enter the adult world before they were ready. They were advised to dress in clothes suitable to their age:

> You'll be a teenager only once so make the most of it.
> Fashion designers are thinking of you these days and the teenage girl has never had it so good.
> These fashions are young and brilliant and this is the only time in your life when you'll be able to wear them.[25]

Through such campaigns, the fashion industries set out to shape 'what interests teenage girls', as 'youthful femininity' rather than simply as 'woman'.

By the mid-1950s, various articles and advertisements in newspapers and women's magazines appeared, instructing teenagers on how to

Fig. 10 Teenage fashions in the 1960s. 'Teenage Whacky Fashions'
was the newspaper caption for this photograph of British teenagers
(*Daily Telegraph*, 28 October 1963).

be 'good consumers'. Articles on using hire-purchase schemes, on
how to look after 'your first pay packet' and on 'planning a teenage
wardrobe' sought to train them not just in how to manage their
money but in thinking of themselves as consumers.[26] Major banks
directed advertising campaigns at 'present-day girls' and 'modern
girls', welcoming their business as a group who, according to the
rhetoric of their advertisements, would, of course, already know
how to regulate their spending.[27] Similarly, the appearance in the
later 1950s of the teenage doll with the long-leggy look of the teenage-
girl shape encouraged young women to think about and take pleasure
in buying a range of fashions appropriate to different occasions.
This was not a doll to be nurtured but to be dressed in a variety of
outfits – a commodity to be collected and surrounded with other
commodities.[28]

This training of young women in 'the importance of having'
complemented the more general rhetoric of advertisers and other
agents of the fashion industries. Together they encouraged young
women to understand themselves as participants in and beneficiaries

of the modern world. The version of modernity thereby sold to them was of a world of abundance in which the ever-changing nature of fashions spoke of that abundance, as well as of a world which was constantly in flux. Modernity, too, was about a democratic world in which all could transform themselves and their appearance through the wealth of goods now available. And it was a world in which the forces which constantly changed and shaped everyday life were a benevolent, domesticated science and a range of industries anxious to fulfil all private hopes and desires. In this context, young women were told they could be involved in modernity as something benign and human as well as exciting and pleasurable.

Not all young women, of course, could have access to this world in the same way. Though they might be addressed by these popular discourses as a single or unified group – young women enjoying the benefits of growing up in the modern world – differences in material circumstances reflecting their class, race and ethnic background did not automatically disappear. But the rhetoric of the consumer culture sought to address them as if they could be identified as one group and to augment and shape their needs and aspirations in this form to be part of the democracy of glamour. Most importantly, it set out to influence the ways in which they evaluated their lives, at the same time as it worked to make them dissatisfied with things as they are and to want access to this world of modernity.[29] Henri Lefebvre depicts the consumer culture of the 1950s as making women the victims of everyday life; women, he claimed, became 'bogged down in its cloying substance' or sought to 'escape into make believe'. Mica Nava, on the other hand, argues that the consumer culture provides women with a new form of agency: it produces new capacities and skills as they learn to become 'good consumers' with an associated set of responsibilities and powers.[30] The next section of this chapter begins to address these questions as it looks further at the sorts of trainings young women were receiving through the rhetoric mobilized by the consumer culture around the space of the teenage girl.

Disciplining the feminine

Janice Winship, writing about English women's magazines in the 1950s and 1960s, argues that these publications promoted an 'individuality' for women which relied on consumption and new forms of work: of beauty, domesticity and child-care. It involved, she says, 'at one and the same time a move towards independence from men and, in its display in an ultimately feminine mould, a repetition of traditional dependence on, and subordination to, men'.[31] This work of femininity required women to learn to make finer and finer distinctions about the sorts of commodities they should use, and surround themselves with, if they were to attain this individuality.

Australian magazine and newspaper articles directed at the young female market in this period concentrated increasingly on the work of glamour and charm – on the skills and techniques involved in presenting their bodies and selves in appropriate feminine form. *The Teenagers' Weekly* exhorted girls to study its articles carefully and to follow instructions. 'It's not just good luck – it's good management', they were told in a 1959 article. Well-groomed and good-looking hair required 'a lot of work',[32] as did their general deportment – the way in which the young woman walked, held her head and sat (crossing her legs or feet neatly to one side, depending on how tall she was).[33] 'Step-by-step' instructions became a popular format in magazines and newspapers for telling them about 'the art of being feminine'. 'Femininity', according to an article in the magazine *New Idea*, required 'diligent work' on skin, hair, eyes, voice, body shape and make-up to produce 'a luminous new you': 'Femininity is not a girlish giggle and a blue hair ribbon. It is simply everything it takes to be a girl . . . sweetness (of person and of personality), naturalness, gaiety, freshness, cleanliness and grace.'[34]

Image was all important. Magazines told girls about ways of changing their personalities – a matter that relied on presentation of their bodies and selves. New hair colours could make you 'a sultry siren', the 'girl next door', the 'moonlight lady' or 'carefree and casual'.[35] Feature articles and advertisements kept girls well-informed about the latest techniques and technologies invented just for them to assist in the presentation of their bodies in appropriate form, such as the new 'step-in' – a special girdle or foundation garment designed for the teenage girl. Training their inner selves was just as important as the transformation of the body, and again techniques of presentation were all important. The concept of charm spoke of a personality which was 'all female': 'Charm . . . is a combination of several fundamental qualities the most important in a woman being femininity – a woman cannot be charming unless she is feminine.' And this femininity had to infuse everything the young woman did, thought and felt: 'Skilful make-up and clever dressing are not enough. Personality and the way it is expressed through speech, manners and general behaviour are equally important.'[36]

Poise, the appearance of confidence, being relaxed and attractiveness were all qualities of charm. This management of the emotions and projection of an inner personality defined a presence guaran-

Teen-age Quest Candidates

"MISS TEEN-AGE' quest candidates are receiving instruction in deportment at a mannequin training academy. In this picture are, L. to R.: Misses Kay Wallis (Miss Armadale), Margaret Kelly (Miss Werribee) and Maria Taranto (Miss Oakleigh). Instructresses are: Misses M. O'Sullivan (principal) and Rita Lloyd.

Fig. 11 Presentation of body and self in feminine form. Beauty quest candidates receiving training in deportment and the correct angle at which to hold their heads (*Age*, 8 March 1950).

teed to please, to put others at their ease and to pose no challenge. 'Charm schools' flourished by the late 1950s, offering to teach young women all they needed to know about these techniques of presentation of their bodies and personalities.

Representations of the male gaze were central to the trainings provided for young women in these contexts. Fashion advertisements often depicted a female model observed by a male figure. At times that gaze was mentioned explicitly in the text – 'It's a man's world this Easter in the realm of feminine holiday clothes'; while other advertisements simply assumed the female reader's desire to be observed by that gaze. Feature articles in the print media instructed young women on the importance of being ever-ready to be watched from every angle. An article in the *Sydney Morning Herald*, for example, spoke of 'the man higher up' looking at you while you sit at work, 'the man beside you' looking at you when you sit beside him at the cinema or restaurant, and 'the man behind you' looking as you sit on a bus or train.[37]

Not only were young women to learn to imagine themselves as always observed – uncertain whether or not they were, but always ready for that gaze – they were also being taught to be constantly anxious about the precise nature of men's desires, of the criteria men used when observing women. Feature articles about film stars discussed whether or not men were changing their preferences – from, for instance, the blonde hair and curvaceous shape of Marilyn Monroe to the slim and long-legged image of Kay Kendall.[38] Other articles assured young women that, in fact, it was not the colour of their hair, the shape of their breasts or the length of their legs that interested men, but their careful attention to their essential femininity, to grace and charm.[39]

These advertisements and feature articles constituted a set of trainings through which the fashion industries and the consumer culture, more generally, sought to invoke in young women the constant desire to be making and remaking their bodies and selves. Imagining themselves continually observed by a gaze whose viewpoint or desires one could never know or control, young women were to learn to take on that gaze themselves. They had to acquire the technique of constantly watching themselves, keeping both their bodies and selves under close scrutiny and unremitting surveillance. Every detail had to be regulated and managed, according to the instructions they were receiving. And, always, they were to be dissatisfied with how they looked, uncertain whether they were making themselves in the right image.

These techniques of self-presentation were portable. As a woman, it was no longer sufficient to learn the skills required to perform the duties in the home of wife and mother; the modern feminine, according to the consumer culture, entailed acquiring a set of attributes which could be transported into any context. The gendered skills involved in grace and charm were to enhance the environment of the home, but they were also of key importance in the modern working place. Young women received advice in the print media about how to prepare themselves for their first job interview in terms of learning the skills of self-presentation in appropriate feminine form. Feature articles about 'working girls' insisted that they needed to know about the 'judicious use of make-up', about how not to 'overdress', the techniques of 'good grooming', and about the workplace etiquette required of a young woman – about how to be polite, friendly, attentive, patient, cheerful, demure, gracious: 'Your office "face" should be cheerful at all times, intelligent,

You—From His Angle

The Man Higher Up →

PROBABLY the position in which your boss sees you most, is when you're taking dictation, with your head bent over your pad. The perfect secretary will be sure her hair is immaculately groomed and her make-up is blended up to the hairline.

Her eyebrows and lashes will be free from powder, and there'll be no smudges on her eye make-up—which will be applied sparingly. Neither will there be unattractive frown lines across her forehead. If she wears glasses, she will have chosen attractively-shaped frames, exactly right for her face.

←The Man Beside You

THINK hard about the last time you saw a girl with her make-up ending at her chin. You probably saw her profile—and this is the way your boy friend sees it in a restaurant, cinema or theatre. Foundation must be smoothed on to the neck and ears (which, of course, are scrupulously clean), then lightly touched with powder.

Check on eyebrow pencil—no harsh line should be visible. Try using one of the new grey pencils for a really natural line, and apply with short, feathery strokes.

If there are signs of a double chin, you'll do well to remember always to keep your head up and back. Of course, this improves posture, too.

Bewitching Italian Summer Charm for YOU!!

Be irresistible this summer. Be gay. Be admired. At Continental Bags a shipment of irresistibly gay and flattering straw Summer bags has arrived. Come soon— very soon. We have now the richest choice of the year.

The Man → Behind You

YOU'RE very much on view from the back, sitting in a bus or train. Tell-tale signs of a slapdash girl are wispy hair ends and a grey neck from wearing sweaters and scarves.

Dandruff is the biggest letdown, especially when it's over the coat collar. Begin treatment for this at once.

If pinching clip-on ear-rings worry you, don't pad with cotton-wool (this always shows), wear special pads.

Fig. 12 Representations of the male gaze. Trainings in the presentation of the body and self in feminine form – always ready to be observed, watched (*Sydney Morning Herald*, 6 August 1956).

alert – and with a clean-cut look that spells efficiency.'[40] These instructions about the necessity for young women to develop gendered skills for the workplace spoke of their Otherness in the world of work. Such skills were said to be in demand in areas like secretarial work, retailing and nursing, as well as in unskilled work in factories. Employed predominantly in occupations where 'feminine skills' were in demand, but expected also to take those skills with them into any workplace, no matter the nature of the job, young women were being told that theirs was a different presence in the paid workforce.[41] They could not simply be 'workers', they had to be first and foremost 'women' to be acceptable in that sphere.

Campaigns to attract young women into particular professions similarly served to underline this conceptual dissonance between 'woman' and 'worker'. Organizations like banks and major retailers set out to attract young women into their workforce by advertising the social life, the leisure facilities, opportunities for travel, the glamour of the job and the attractive uniforms provided. 'Modern conditions' also featured as an important aspect of the attractions of particular jobs, defined by descriptions of the decor of offices or staff canteens and by the equipment to be used. For instance, qualified nurses were in short supply and many changes were introduced in the conditions surrounding their work throughout the 1950s and early 1960s in the attempt to attract more young women into the profession. But it was the social life, the uniforms, the rooms in which they lived, which were transformed (and commended in the media), rather than the actual conditions of the work itself – such as the hours or the pay. 'New Look' uniforms, accommodation which was made more 'homely' and 'modern' compared to the institutional arrangements of the past, and opportunities for overseas travel featured in advertisements and newspaper reports on the benefits of becoming a nurse. Equal pay battles went on throughout this period, but questions about the conditions of nurses' work and their levels of pay only began to be acknowledged in media reports of the nursing shortage in the mid-1960s.[42] Campaigns to recruit young women into the workforce assumed their interest in work not to be, first and foremost, as potential workers, but as young women whose interests could be encapsulated in an image of the modern feminine: a streamlined, efficient femininity whose interests lay in attractive modern conditions, a good social life, and glamour. These expectations about a femininity designed to please in the presentation of body and self reinforced the trainings young women were receiving through the media and the advertising campaigns of the clothing and cosmetics industries.

Iris Marion Young in her paper 'Throwing like a girl' analyses what she refers to as the modalities of feminine bodily existence. She points to 'a specific positive style of feminine body comportment and movement, which is learned as the girl comes to understand that she is a girl'.[43] Young women learn, she argues, to live their bodies as object as well as subject. They actively take up the position of treating and looking at their own bodies as mere things as they come to recognize that an

> essential part of the situation of being a woman is that of
> living the ever present possibility that one will be gazed upon

as mere body, as shape and flesh that presents itself as the potential object of another subject's intentions and manipulations, rather than as living manifestation of action and intention.[44]

Young suggests a connection between these forms of trainings which shape the modalities of feminine bodily existence and other aspects of the existence and experience of women. As an example, she hypothesizes a link between a general lack of confidence among women in their cognitive and leadership abilities and a doubt about the capacities of their bodies to act upon the world, to engage in the world's possibilities.[45]

Instructions to young women about the presentation of their bodies and selves in the Australian print media and advertising campaigns of the 1950s and early 1960s illustrate vividly Young's account of the forms of training received by women in the process of their learning what it means to be a woman. This publicity material carried constant messages, as I have described above, about the 'subtle habits of feminine comportment' referred to by Young: the requirements of 'walking like a girl, tilting her head like a girl, standing and sitting like a girl, gesturing like a girl'.[46] But this historical evidence also suggests that Young does not acknowledge sufficiently the changing nature of this education, nor does she consider whether this education may be, now or in the past, class differentiated.[47] Though she stresses at the beginning of her paper that she is not analysing some natural and ahistorical feminine essence in specifying the modalities of the lived female body, but the unity of women's experiences produced by a given socio-historical set of circumstances,[48] she fails to place that history at the centre of her analysis.

The material I have been looking at in this chapter suggests a significant change in the post-Second World War period in the forms of trainings provided to young women as a group. Defining the space of the teenage girl as the time in their lives when young women learnt to produce their bodies in feminine form, the commercial culture of the 1950s and 1960s gave public visibility and a new emphasis to a set of trainings which had in the past been class differentiated and primarily conducted in the privacy of the home, the ladies' school or particular working environments. These former modes of instruction continued to exist in schools, gymnasium classes and no doubt in many homes, but in the 'democracy of glamour' all young women were now expected and provided with the appropriate information and technologies through the consumer culture to make their bodies according to a single set of norms – the norms

RIGHT WAY... AND THE WRONG

RIGHT: Judy McBurney shows the short girl look.

WRONG: Lee Thompson demonstrates the "legs entwined."

RIGHT: Tana Bindon and the tall girl party look.

WRONG: Janet Naismith shows the arms akimbo sprawl.

RIGHT: June Dally-Watkins, the sophisticate.

EXPERT TIPS ON HOW TO 'SIT PRETTY'

Sydney women worried about their "platform image" can take heart from the ruling of a leading authority on deportment.

There are at least four ways a girl can sit, even in a short, tight skirt, and still remain a lady!

Miss June Dally-Watkins, head of a Sydney school of deportment demonstrated for "The Sun-Herald" this week the right and the wrong way to sit.

With a group of model girls, Miss Dally-Watkins illustrated:

● The business girl "sit."
● The tall girl party

● The short girl party look.
● The ultra-sophisticate look.

And, to show what not to do:

● The legs-entwined "sit."
● The arms akimbo sprawl.
● The chair leg hook.

Miss Dally-Watkins was commenting on an attack on "platform" posture made

this week by a Chatswood woman.

In a letter to "The Sydney Morning Herald," the woman said:

"Before Christmas and at the breaking-up of the school term, I was present at four speech day/night gatherings.

of the fashion industry and its associated agents, the beauty consultants and charm schools. These developments in the post-Second
World War period worked precisely to produce the unity of experience of which Young speaks as characterizing the modalities
of feminine bodily existence, but at a very particular historical
moment.

Yet they did so in ways which were far more contradictory than
Young's analysis of the possible significance of these forms of training
for women implies. I want to point to two apparent paradoxes in
the ways in which the space of the teenage girl was being delineated
at this time. First, Young argues that, to the extent that women
learn to live out their existence according to these definitions of the
feminine, they become 'physically inhibited, confined, positioned,
and objectified'.[49] While Young depicts the norms of female comportment as something which only a few fortunate women have
managed to avoid or overcome, I want to look instead at the norms
themselves as producing tensions which ensured their inability to
operate totally successfully in all women's lives. Instructions to young
women, such as those in the 'step-by-step' format which became
very popular in magazines like *The Teenagers' Weekly* or *New Idea* in
the late 1950s and early 1960s, set out to teach them about how to
be 'essentially feminine'; yet the very proliferation of this information and the variousness of the images of femininity they invoked
spoke of its belonging to a world of surfaces. If it was now possible
for young women to transform themselves from the 'girl-next-door'
into the 'sultry siren' (or vice versa) simply by changing their hair
colour, then it became possible also to understand femininity as
nothing more than a question of the image itself. Indeed, if different
images of femininity could be taken on and off, then so too, by
implication, could femininity itself.[50]

Simone de Beauvoir, in a portrait of the French film actress, Brigitte
Bardot, published in English in 1959, provoked questions along this
line in the Australian press when her short book about this young
star was reviewed at the beginning of 1961. De Beauvoir wrote ad-
miringly of Bardot as departing significantly from the vamp image
of movie stars like Marlene Dietrich who, she argued, exercised
attraction over men by presenting themselves and their bodies as
passive objects. Bardot, she claimed, 'is on the go'; her clothes are
not fetishes speaking of the mystery of her body; her eroticism is

---

Fig. 13 The feminine body. Trainings in the modalities of feminine
bodily existence (a report on the June Dally-Watkins' Deportment
School, Sydney) (*Sun-Herald*, 14 February 1965).

aggressive and 'the male is an object to her, just as she is to him'.[51] De Beauvoir analysed the unease that Bardot appeared to create among at least some male audiences as demonstrating how her sexuality claimed her equal with men. Spurning the accoutrements of feminine fashions, cosmetics and jewellery, Bardot expressed her own sexuality, de Beauvoir argued, rather than waiting passively to be the object of masculine desire. Nan Hutton, reviewing the book in the Melbourne *Age*, dismissed this interpretation, however, as failing to acknowledge that Bardot herself was 'putting on the Bardot act'. Her uncombed hair, her refusal of jewels and cosmetics and shoes, and her tight pants and sweaters, Hutton suggested, was just as much a pose as any other image of femininity.[52]

On a less serious level, press stories about the changing shape of young womanhood also pointed to the instability of notions of 'the essential feminine'. A feature article in the *Sun-Herald* in 1956 headed 'Shape of Girls to Come', for instance, reported the research of a foundation garment company which suggested Australian girls were now two inches taller, two inches slimmer around the waist, had added two inches to their busts and had larger feet than their counterparts of the 1930s. The writer pondered whether the prospect of average Australian girls growing taller might not be a frightening one: 'Does it mean', he asked, that the Australian male 'will be faced with a race of Amazons who will outpace, outgrow, outrule and outvote him?'[53]

If 'the essential feminine' could not be specified clearly or unambiguously and femininity itself could be put on and taken off at will, then the possibility emerged that women could, or already had, become aware of the distance between a self which they sensed as existing somehow separate from, as Mary Ann Doane puts it, their 'own' fully feminized gestures.[54] The trainings I have been describing which sought to show young women how to manage their bodies, emotions and selves according to fashionable notions of 'the essential feminine', were also lessons in how to disengage gesture from essence. Beauty secrets told 'woman to woman', yet in the public setting of the woman's magazine or the woman's or teenage section of the newspaper, spoke of artifice, but also of some form of farce as everyone 'really knew' that femininity was a mask to be put on or taken off at will. The possibility, of which Iris Marion Young speaks, that some women might appear to ignore or somehow avoid the norms of femininity promulgated in such contexts, arises then not through some accidental release or individual quirk of a few; it is produced precisely by the tensions surrounding these norms as they were increasingly delineated in the 1950s. The emphasis placed on the anxious but calculating cultivation of appearance which

emerged in this period, simultaneously made it possible to understand femininity as not defining some essential truth of womanhood
but as a mask to be changed, reworked, manipulated and discarded,
if so desired.[55]

The second paradox I want to point to concerns the instructions
young women received which spoke of the female body as in need
of disguise, transformation and containment. The body which is
always ready for the male gaze, watching itself from every angle, is
contained, keeping itself very much 'under control'. Mikhail Bakhtin
contrasts what he refers to as the modern bodily canon of the closed,
completed body with the grotesque body which, he argues, is
constantly growing, transgressing itself and its own limits. This latter
body is an unfinished body and it is open to the world, rather than
closed in upon itself.[56] The image of the teenage girl as 'all arms and
legs' intimated a bodily existence which was unfinished and open,
in these terms. Penny, the comic strip character described in Chapter 6, exemplified this image when she was depicted as lying on the
family sofa with her legs in the air in carnivalesque fashion, as she
talked on the telephone to her friends.[57] The teenage girl received
instructions 'as a woman' on how to manage her body, to make it
contained and closed off. Yet, the emphasis on the figure of the
teenage girl as a distinctive one with its own shape and ways sat
uneasily with these notions that the young woman was always
already a woman and her growing up simply involved learning
what that meant. Though public spokesmen like John Medley, the
educationalist, expressed some anxiety about 'teenagers wanting to
remain teenagers', the consumer industries increasingly throughout
the 1950s and 1960s attempted to augment and encourage young
women's desires to take pleasure in doing precisely just that. They
were being persuaded to understand themselves as 'teenage girls'
with their own modes of bodily comportment (and hence their own
fashions to express their distinctive ways of being-in-the-world) and
to want to remain 'teenagers' for ever-extending periods of their life.

Mary Russo draws attention to the concerns which underlie
Bakhtin's counterposing of what he describes as the modern bodily
canon with the grotesque body and, more generally, the culture
of the carnival which he sees as having existed in early modern
Europe. His work, she says,

> contains a critique of modernity and its stylistic effects as a
> radical diminishment of the possibilities of human freedom
> and cultural production. He considers the culture of modern-
> ity to be as austere and bitterly isolating as the official reli-
> gious culture of the Middle Ages, which he contrasts with the

joy and heterogeneity of carnival and the carnivalesque style
and spirit.[58]

Training young women in the modalities of feminine bodily existence so that they learnt to place themselves in the world as object
rather than subject would appear to involve such a 'radical dimin-
ishment of the possibilities of human freedom and cultural production'. To be constantly working to produce one's body and self in
feminine form which is closed off, under control, ready to be viewed
as an object and whose point is to please another, speaks of an
existence which is itself closed off, limited to a narrow set of concerns. Though young women were told to seek constantly to make
and remake themselves in desirable form by the consumer culture,
this process was to be very much directed towards a specific end.
The point of learning to produce their bodies and selves in a particular form was so that they could attract and catch the man they
would marry.

But to argue this case is not to accept Henri Lefebvre's depiction
of women as victims of the consumer culture which becomes so
powerful in the 1950s in reorganizing everyday life. These trainings
sought to produce a particular way of being-in-the-world for women
which entailed an immense amount of anxiety and a sense of oneself as always dissatisfied in its implications of a constant need to
observe, scrutinize and keep one's body and self 'under control'. But
they also produced the possibility of a set of pleasures around a
certain sort of playfulness about one's identity, about the sort of
woman one might 'truly' be. This contradiction or tension would
itself be productive of ways of being-in-the-world which could
create the possibility that at least some young women would not
understand and learn fully or successfully to place themselves in the
world simply as objects. Further, these sets of trainings in this
'democracy of glamour' spoke of a category of 'woman', of 'woman's
desire', which would have contradictory effects in the late 1960s
and early 1970s: in its production of a publicly available and identifiable sense of shared needs and experiences of women 'as a group',
it would provide the basis for women to mobilize against the forces
in society which sought to contain and diminish the possibilities
of their being and becoming many different things 'as women'.
Finally, the trainings of the teenage girl which spoke of a bodily
existence which was 'all arms and legs' suggested a process of self-
making that for a time at least was more open-ended, playful,
ambivalent, than a growing up which represented that period in
one's life as simply a question of recognizing oneself to be always
already a woman.

The final section of this chapter looks at how the popular media in this period formulated the story of the young woman's engagement in the tasks of growing up as having its end, its necessary point of closure, in marriage. But it investigates, too, some of the other accounts of young women growing up that also circulated in these same contexts and which gave them public visibility in this form.

Feminine achievement stories

The importance of marriage in a young woman's life assumed the status of a taken-for-granted understanding in the popular magazines and in the feature sections in the daily press directed at the teenage girl. The primary purpose of young women learning to make their bodies and self in appropriate feminine form, according to the rhetoric of these publications, was to prepare for the moment when they would meet the man they would marry, the potential dreamed-about lover. Though young women were to carry these gendered skills into the workplace and wherever they moved, their central preoccupation was always depicted as meeting, attracting and catching the man that would make them 'the loved individual'. Instructions about how to prepare oneself for this moment in one's life provided one of the major themes of popular feature articles for the teenage girl.

Conduct books also proliferated in this period similarly geared to assisting the young woman to ensure that her growing up did come to a satisfactory conclusion. These appear to have been published predominantly by church organizations or affiliated bodies. Some concentrated on the 'facts of life' – on sex education – others on 'the art of dating', but all discussed what they represented as the natural difficulties and pleasures of being an adolescent on 'the threshold of life' and all assumed that on the other side of that threshold lay marriage and a life of being a wife and mother.[59] Even the apparently outrageously different publication by Helen Gurley Brown, *Sex and the Single Girl*, published in 1963, and considered outrageous by many at the time, conformed essentially to these concerns. Gurley Brown made much more of the work involved in producing one's self and body in feminine form ready for the right man to come along, and she urged young women to enjoy and prolong their single status for some time, but all of these activities and pleasures were to be geared to achieving and being properly prepared for the status of marriage.[60]

While these publications and the popular media advice columns shared the concern that young women prepare themselves for marriage, they were also adamant that they should not seek to attain that status too soon. The categories of adolescence and teenagerhood played a key role in this advice, claiming the necessity of waiting, of preparation, and of a proper period of growing up before young women declared themselves ready for marriage and began a period of 'serious dating'. Young women were warned not to have emotional involvements during their teenage years and not to be active sexually. Detailed instructions were provided about the limits they should place on how much physical and social contact to have with 'the opposite sex': 'be calm and sensible and you'll soon grow up'.[61] But they were assured, too, that they should be provided with sufficient and appropriate space by their parents in which to do this growing up. One 15 year-old-girl writing to the 'agony column' in *New Idea*, for instance, was told:

> As you know, your father is trying to protect you, but it's just as important that he learns to trust you. The days when fathers locked their daughters up in ivory towers have long since passed. You must be allowed to learn to take your place in the world. Sitting with boys in the pictures at your age is OK providing you are part of a group, not just cuddly twosomes.[62]

Parents received this same advice: of the necessity to keep their eyes on their daughters while also allowing the appropriate degree of freedom necessary for them 'to grow up successfully' in the modern world.

This notion of the necessity of a space of supervised freedom for modern girls defined a group of individuals on the threshold of adulthood, but needing time to grow up, to be an adolescent. The purpose of this time out in this context was not, however, to pursue the tasks of making a self, the tasks of the modern individual; it was a space in which the young woman was supposed to discover in herself heterosexual desires, to be troubled by those desires, but to learn that they were to be managed, kept under control. Parents, in this story of growing up, no longer were responsible for keeping their daughters pure until the time that they entered an arranged marriage. Modern young women had to learn to find in themselves the desire for marriage and to learn the rules of conducting their relations with men so as to ensure they achieved this end. 'A proper growing up' in this context involved the discovery in oneself of an increasing awareness of (hetero)sexual desires (which biology would supposedly of necessity produce) and a learning to control those desires for their 'proper purpose' to be expressed in marriage.

Newspaper headlines about 'the child bride evil' in the late 1950s, served to draw attention to the dangers of young women not learning the last of these lessons. Various legal, psychological and medical professionals spoke of the problems of young people marrying at too young an age, claiming that such early marriages would lead to unhappiness and divorce. Reports from the USA confirmed this picture with statistics provided in 1959, for instance, claiming that marriages of girls between the ages of 14 and 17 had increased by one-third over the previous few years, and three out of five of these marriages were believed to have ended in divorce. 'Shot-gun marriages' came under attack in Australia with claims by social workers and church spokespersons that most of the 'child bride' marriages occurred because the young woman was pregnant.[63] The federal government brought in legislation to cover all states in 1960 to raise the legal age of marriage to 16 for girls and 18 for boys (as well as seeking to change notions of the legitimacy of children born out of wedlock). The popular press and conduct books defined young people as a separate category of person by depicting them as sexual beings possessing an awakening sexuality which had to be contained, held in waiting until maturity, and thereby guided in appropriate directions. These legal reforms and the publicity leading up to them defined the consequences and the dangers of that sexuality being allowed 'out of control', thus giving greater force to the claims being made in a range of other settings of the importance of young women remaining 'young people', adolescents, for a specific period of time. Though the story of their growing up had a clearly defined point of closure in all these settings, they were expected to accept social norms about when the appropriate time would come for them to end that process.

Accounts of the 'child bride evil' provided dramatic opportunity to warn young women of the necessity for extreme caution in their management of their desires in order to draw the narrative of their growing up to a satisfactory conclusion. Two major cultural institutions of the 1950s and 1960s, however, were much more concerned with celebrating and giving public visibility to the young woman's declaration of herself as being ready to take on the status of adult womanhood. The appeal to young women by the consumer culture to make their bodies into particular female forms through purchasing the clothes and other beauty aids provided by the market worked on the suggestion that 'existing' in one's body entailed choice, interpretation and achievement. Debutante balls and beauty contests of this period served to draw attention to this sense of femininity as achievement, at the same time as they worked to contain and limit how it was understood. These events celebrated the feminine qualities of glamour, poise, a figure correctly proportioned and a

Fig. 14 Feminine achievement stories: The debutante. A local
debutante ball, Newcastle 1955.

charming personality, but they also constituted social spaces of visibility or public presence for a story of feminine achievement.

Media reports of debutante balls depicted young women making
their curtsies to local or more prominent dignitaries, declaring
themselves ready 'to come out'. Some girls were fortunate enough to
be presented to the Queen, while others could feel like 'princesses'
in 'sumptuous settings, breath-taking gowns and dazzling jewels',
and always, they were 'a delight to the eye'.[64] Adolescent femininity
– the young woman growing up, declaring herself ready for adult
womanhood – received recognition, acquired a radiant visibility in
this form. But this story of achievement, of a young woman making
herself, also announced her tasks of growing up completed. Her
'coming out' was the traditional ritual of her declared readiness for
marriage; she announced herself 'woman' and her desire to relinquish her responsibility for the tasks of making herself to engage
instead in the pleasures of becoming 'the loved individual'.

Similarly, the beauty quest told a story of feminine achievement
at the same time as it affirmed the necessity of marriage as providing

the goal of this project and its desired point of closure. Contests like Miss Australia, Miss Teenage and Miss International Beauty received the most publicity in the daily press and women's magazines, but many others sponsored by diverse organizations appeared in the photographs and news columns of these publications: The Mildura Raisin Beauty Queen of 1955, the Trade Union Queen of 1953, the Queen of the Air of 1951, for example, all received publicity in the Melbourne *Age*. Similarly, the many entrants for Miss Teenage of Victoria were photographed in the press and the winner appeared each year on the front page of the major Melbourne newspapers. Quest winners were those most successful in learning the lessons that surrounded them. They had achieved through acquiring the techniques of self-monitoring and the continual surveillance of their bodies and personalities, and through learning to choose and use in expert manner the fashion commodities provided for them. Successful contestants expressed excitement at their achievement being acknowledged and celebrated in words typically about 'the thrill' of it all, of it being '. . . all like a dream'.[65]

Occasional criticisms of the beauty quests interrupted or disturbed the legitimacy of these images of female success. In 1950, a spate of criticisms appeared in the press, provoked by the apparent contrariness of Miss Australia herself. She had refused the services of the chaperon officially provided for her, preferring to choose her own. In response, an *Age* editorial asked whether these competitions did 'more harm than good to the young womanhood of the nation'. It went on to suggest that: 'Happy, unselfconscious womanhood in the home, at work or at play, is always to be admired in the proper setting under suitable conditions, but ostentatious display for its own sake is to be deprecated.'[66]

Letters to the editor similarly joined in with criticisms of the beauty quest as removing women from 'their homely joys and destiny obscure'.[67] These comments raised the spectre of beauty contests sponsoring a femininity taking pleasure simply in itself, a 'femininity out-of-control'. But this setback in 1950 was followed in future years by a growing number of competitions receiving publicity as a celebration of femininity whose point lay outside itself. It was a femininity to be looked at for the pleasure of others and it was a feminine achievement story looking for an appropriate end – in marriage.

Interviews with beauty quest winners frequently mentioned marriage, an engagement postponed or the absence of plans 'for the present'.[68] The most successful beauty contestant was also most adored by the daily press for providing a very straightforward image of this tale of feminine achievement looking for an appropriate ending.

Miss Teenager of 1955

● MARGARET MAD-
DER, who was an-
nounced the winner of
the 3AW Miss Teen-
age Quest by the
Governor (Sir Dallas
Brooks) in the Town
Hall last night, is con-
gratulated by other
contestants. Included
in the first prize is a
trip to Hollywood. All
proceeds go to 3AW's
Royal Women's Hospi-
tal appeal.

Fig. 15 Feminine achievement stories: The beauty queen. Miss
Teenager of 1955 (Victoria) (*Age*, 5 May 1955).

Tania Verstak, winner of Miss Australia in 1961 and crowned Miss International Beauty in a 'glittering ceremony' at Long Beach in California in August 1962, was just 'an ordinary girl', who, the *Sun-Herald* announced shortly after her international victory, was 'ready – anytime – to fall in love and marry'.[69] She achieved her desire less than a year later and became 'Mrs Peter Young', pictured in the press as 'the world's most glamorous housewife'.[70]

The figure of Tania Verstak played a number of roles in the Australian media in the early 1960s. Her story could be recruited very readily to a tale of the desirability of youth – the time in which a person is involved in making a self – as being a period in a person's life which is necessarily circumscribed. While travelling overseas, she constantly spoke of her desire to return 'home', at the same time as she insisted that she recognized the wonderful opportunities given to her by this experience of glamour and achievement. Similarly, her success was used to place limits on the story of femininity as achievement: as an 'ordinary girl' her femininity was not an end in itself but was directed at attaining true feminine fulfilment in the roles of wife and mother.

However, other themes were also mobilized around her success in the popular media and in the official discourses of government spokespersons. Tania Verstak was an immigrant, born in China of White Russian parents, who came to Australia after the Chinese communist revolution. The victory of a 'new Australian' in an Australian beauty quest, as well as overseas, symbolized a new image of nationhood which Federal parliamentarians sought to recruit by proposing she was already and should be made officially an 'ambassadress' for a new image of Australia. She was commended for her contribution to international goodwill: 'she has been an ambassadress as charming as she has been valuable'. And she was claimed to be 'with such success and distinction, . . . an example of what a young person coming here as a migrant can achieve in a relatively short space of time'.[71]

Miss Australia contestants travelling overseas had increasingly in the late 1950s been referred to as 'ambassadresses' for the nation: youthful, feminine loveliness as an image of a young nation full of hope and promise. Tania Verstak, however, played an important additional role in providing a symbol of resolution to a troubled image of the nation within Australia. As an immigrant she was retained as different; but as demure, gracious femininity she fitted in, was a pleasure to have 'among us'. Images of young female migrants had played this role throughout the 1950s. The immigration programme in Australia in the post-Second World War period

(a)

Fig. 16 Feminine achievement stories: The beauty queen and the happy ending to the story. (a) 'Miss Australia 1961', Tania Verstak. (b) Miss Australia now 'Mrs Peter Young' (*Sun-Herald*, 17 March 1963).

constituted a major modernization project, launched by the Federal Labor Government in 1948 to provide a massive boost to the labour force. By the end of 1963, about two million migrants had arrived since the war.[72] Popular support for this project of modernization was by no means eagerly given. While images of masculinity featured in celebrations of the modernization projects of building dams and power stations – man taming nature, making us master of the world – images of innocent, youthful femininity (the migrant

(b)

girl) served to defuse the sense of threat, the sense of the foreign as dangerous in a project which would transform the social and cultural character of Australia. 'New land – new home – new hopes for Elizabeth' declared one newspaper in its caption for a photo of a pretty young woman. In 1955, a young woman from Yorkshire in England was conveniently the millionth post-war migrant.[73] Tania Verstak symbolized the immigrant as now firmly placed within the nation, but she also was the good, virtuous immigrant, the immigrant whose only desire was to please and to be pleasing.

The increasing recruitment of the public visibility of youthful femininity to images of modern nationhood in media accounts of the beauty quest in the 1950s and 1960s reworked and exploited a theme which had emerged in the early 1950s around various members of the British royal family. At the beginning of the 1950s, 'the young princesses' – Elizabeth and Margaret – were key figures in the mobilization of an image of a youthful, modern nationhood for Australia. As 'ordinary girls' who enjoyed wearing 'the latest fashions', they provided a sense of its place in a new world in which citizenship could be symbolized by youthful, feminine charm.[74] Australia could now hold its own and its population could likewise enjoy full citizenship in this new democratic world order that valued youth and modernity.

Princess Margaret continued to play this role for some years. She was pictured wearing the latest fashions, attending fashion parades, dancing and smoking. These pleasures of a modern, everyday feminine were also ones which she was expected to abandon once she turned 21 and the media eagerly awaited her announcement of a planned marriage. But for a while at least, she attracted their attention as a pleasing image of modern citizenship in a world which celebrated and revolved around ordinary, material pleasures. Princess Elizabeth, however, became the young Queen in 1952 with the death of her father, King George VI. On her accession to the throne, she provided an opportunity to celebrate an image of youth as a citizen-in-the-making more concerned with serving the nation than with enjoying the modern way of life. Her tour of Australia in 1954 became a key moment for the Australian print media to celebrate this notion of the relationship between a modern nation and its citizens, while her 'young', 'slim', 'girlish', 'lovely-to-look-at' femininity softened that notion of service. Media reports of the numbers of young people and children welcoming her in cities and country towns signalled her connection to 'the youth of the nation', at the same time as it told a story of a romance between citizens and their nation's leader in which service, being 'loyal subjects', became a question of pleasure and delight rather than a matter of mere duty.[75]

Later in the decade, another visit of British royalty by Princess Alexandra similarly provided ample opportunity for the press to celebrate an image of charming, young, feminine citizenship. Like Margaret, Alexandra symbolized a modern, youthful femininity, but one, in this instance, which, by 1959, had more clearly a shape of its own. Margaret enjoyed the pleasures of modern life available to young women in the 1950s 'democracy of glamour'; Alexandra, however, personified modern youthful femininity with her 'spontaneous', 'natural' gaiety and charm. Her tour was announced as having an 'accent on youth' before her arrival and all reports of her, whether in regal ballgown, riding a horse, or shaking hands with crowds of admirers, emphasized this same feature of her public appearances in Australia.[76] She represented a figure to be admired but also identified with rather than an object of devotion. In this guise, she provided an opportunity for celebrating youthful femininity as a pleasing public presence, at the same time as that image was recruited to a story of modern democratic nationhood in which all could and would want to participate.

Other feminine figures also played this role in the media of constituting a public presence for modern youthful femininity at the same time as they were recruited to this image of nationhood. The successes of female athletes, like Betty Cuthbert, Marlene Matthews and Shirley Strickland, in the 1956 Olympic Games held in Melbourne, provided the media ample opportunity to sing the praises of young Australian womanhood. The youthfulness of these champions was the subject of comment, as was their 'unassuming modesty' and 'fun-loving' normality. Their achievements were celebrated in terms of their 'fresh', 'slim' femininity. Media reports indicated some unease about this link between sport and femininity, but comments by a manager of one of the US women's teams about sport making girls more attractive, more interesting and giving them 'more poise', provided an opportunity to ensure that the appropriate link could be made.[77] Sport was interpreted as a training in femininity and success in this arena became another feminine achievement story like that of the beauty quest winner. Betty Cuthbert provided ample opportunity for the media to provide this type of account of the 'girl victors' in the Olympic Games. The *Age* described her when she received her gold medal as having 'blue eyes which always sparkled', 'a pretty girl' now 'radiant' with 'the world of sport at her feet' whose only desire at the end of the Games was to go off to Luna Park.[78] Youthful femininity acquired a public visibility in this context of a modern, young nation celebrating its victories and the jubilant young women could speak of their pleasure and excitement in their success. But their presence in the media also provided an opportunity for the affirmation of a particular kind of femininity – a femininity guaranteed to please, a femininity-under-control – and their triumphs were celebrated as another instance of young women achieving success as women. In the world of work, young women had to learn that they were present differently; in the world of sport, too, they were depicted as first and foremost sexed identities and their achievement in this arena was to be understood in these terms.

But not all media accounts of youthful femininity could recruit it so securely to notions of a modern democratic nationhood mobilized in various contexts in Australia in the 1950s. In the public rhetoric which surrounded modernization projects in Australia in the early 1950s, the conservative government led by Robert Menzies set out to gain popular support for its policies through a set of campaigns around notions of the need for a convinced citizenry. An aggressive anti-communist stance constituted the central theme of these campaigns, through which the Menzies government constituted an enemy within and without. According to the rhetoric of this propaganda, Australia as a modern democratic nation was under threat from these dangerous forces and only the vigilance and commitment of its citizenry as demonstrated in all aspects of their daily life could save her. Government advertisements appeared in the daily press as part of this campaign depicting women at the centre of family life, attentive to the needs of family and nation.[79] They called on all members of the population, 'men and women, young and old', to make the 'choice of freedom', to make the social order 'their own' through their 'personal decisions to support the Government and its production programmes in the areas of defence and national development'.[80] This propaganda constituted the State, simultaneously, in its traditional form as paternalistic protector of loyal subjects, and as seeking to renew its contract with a modern citizenry of independent individuals 'freely' giving consent to the social order. Woman 'choosing' to play her part in this modern citizenry by performing her duties as mother and wife provided a convenient image of a figure who was at one and the same time a loyal subject and modern citizen. But these images served also to suggest limits on the extent to which women could make a claim for full membership of this citizenry; they had no existence in this context beyond their roles as wife and mother.

But women in the form of the feminine consumer became one of the 'enemies within' in the first few years of this decade. This figure with her 'frivolous' desires for such 'luxury goods' as make-up and nylon garments, according to the Menzies government, threatened national development. Various official spokesmen declared that setting up of factories to produce such items diverted vital national resources away from the establishment of power stations, water supply works and heavy machinery industries.[81] The announcement by the Myer Emporium in Melbourne that they intended to build a new department store in the city of Geelong was criticized in the state parliament as 'a giant luxury building' taking away skilled labour and scarce materials from more important projects.[82] Several Labor politicians attempted to interrupt this official discourse and its implicit gendering of consumption. They criticized the government's tax on 'luxury' items as an attack on the everyday feminine of 'lipstick, powder and face creams' in the interests of protecting the luxuries of the wealthy.

By the late 1950s, however, this everyday feminine had become something which governments urged industry to pursue. The building of Australia's first nylon factory in 1958 was described in the press as heralding a new age of exciting developments for the Australian manufacturing industry.[83] Such reports now welcomed these initiatives as creating jobs and represented women's desires for nylon stockings, lingerie and dress fabrics as well-established and legitimate.[84] Indeed, to fail to notice and serve this modern feminine, according to one industry spokesperson, was to 'commit suicide'. Placing particular emphasis on the young female consumer, he called for the wool industry to adjust itself to 'modern conditions':

> . . . synthetics and cottons are already taking the place of wool, and to pretend otherwise is pathetic self deception. Young girls, for instance, commonly wear cotton blouses and jeans, or for slightly more formal occasions, terylene skirts. They only know wool in its shoddy wartime form, and nobody has taken the trouble to show them its great virtues.[85]

Myer Emporium, too, now received enthusiastic approval for its activities in attending to the needs of the feminine consumer. Newspaper publicity for its plans to open up a Californian-style shopping centre in suburban Melbourne at Chadstone described the complex as a space designed by men for the pleasure and needs of the modern woman.[86] Modernity celebrated and served the everyday feminine, at the same time as it sought to pin it down, know its every desire and whim, in order to make calculations about it for the benefit of the nation.

For the most part, then, the visibility which opened up for the modern feminine in the 1950s and, in particular, to the story of young women growing up, was understood as celebrating and serving a femininity-under-control. Media reports of the activities of young women took particular delight in telling of their achievements when it was clear that the sphere in which they most wanted to succeed was in making themselves ready for adult womanhood. In delineating the space of the modern girl in these terms, accounts of young women growing up also became opportunities to recruit their public presence to various attempts to define Australia as a modern democratic nation and to seek the commitment of its population to these images of nationhood and citizenship. But young women were not thereby granted full citizenship in official or popular rhetoric; they were to be citizens in limited ways only as they prepared themselves for the roles in which they would be accorded such a status – the roles of wife and mother. Events like beauty quests and sporting successes gave young women the opportunity to be seen and heard, but they were to present their bodies and selves in appropriate female form and to speak only in demure, girlish fashion of their desires for homely pleasures. The feminine achievement story in these contexts was necessarily a story looking for an end. The modern world offered the young woman 'the best of everything', but it also assumed her desire for a safe place, a sense of belonging, to be found through devoting her adult life to the roles of wife and mother. These accounts of feminine achievement, of the young woman making her self, recruited the cultural ideal of the self-determining individual to an affirmation and celebration of a normative definition of 'the essential feminine'.

Endings

A ruler measures how tall you are and the school report card shows how bright you are. But how do you tell just how grown up you are?
(*Australian Women's Weekly*, 26 December 1962, p. 3)

The teenage supplement to the *Australian Women's Weekly* offered 16 'signposts' for its young readers to help them answer the question, 'how grown up am I?' These included respecting the company and advice of parents rather than looking always to one's peers, liking to be alone to have the 'privacy to study, read or try new beauty hints' and beginning to 'value responsibility'. '[I]f you've already reached some of the signposts', readers were told, 'you're on the right road to "growing up".' Such advice defined the period of growing up in a young person's life as a time of anxiety and uncertainty. Surrounded by competing influences of parents, teachers and friends, they had to learn to take responsibility for themselves and to do so in the correct manner. There was a 'proper way' to be an adult and a 'proper way' to grow up, but only 'signposts' about the sorts of feelings and desires they should somehow find in themselves, rather than a set of regulations to ensure that they took the right road. Other advice in this or other magazines would at times recommend teenagers to enjoy their youth as 'the best years of your life'.[1] However, the general consensus was that this period of growing up was simply a stage in a young person's life, the meaning and significance of which lay in their eventually achieving a stable and responsible adult identity.

Franco Moretti describes the classical *Bildungsroman* as subordinating youth to the idea of maturity. According to this cultural form, the meaning of the events of youth lies in its leading to a particularly marked ending. The freedom and risks of making, determining, one's own identity – the period of becoming associated with youth – is exchanged for the happiness of belonging, the end of the journey. Similarly, I have sought to show in this book that the advice columns and feature articles directed primarily at a young female readership in the print media of the 1950s and early 1960s began to portray youth as a period of experimentation and growth, at the same time as they claimed it a circumscribed experience, the meaning of which resided in its necessary ending. Young women were encouraged to understand themselves as having characteristic needs and interests as 'teenage girls'. They were urged to enjoy this time in their lives to the full, to take advantage of the pleasures on offer to them, to travel overseas, to experience the adventure and excitement of being youth. But the exhilaration of being 'modern girls' would be relinquished for the happiness of becoming the 'loved individual' of the romance stories also filling the pages of these publications.

I have argued, too, that the normative definitions of growing up circulating within and legitimating the reorganization of the secondary education system in the 1950s and early 1960s, likewise, sought both to augment the period of youth in the lives of all young people and to ensure that it reached a satisfactory point of closure. The increasing authority of psychological expertise in educational settings, as well as in surrounding social welfare and legal institutions, delineated a series of developmental tasks involved in a 'proper growing up' through which the young person would acquire a stable, coherent identity. Growing up entailed making a self in this form; adulthood was the end of this process, as the individual learnt to reconcile what was understood as the adolescent's 'need' for autonomy with the demands of the social world.

And yet, the choices young women were expected to make were gendered. The end of their story of growing up was assumed to involve their taking on the roles of wife and mother or, in rare cases, 'choosing' a career instead. So, too, were the norms of identity formation gendered, as elaborated in the context of the modernized secondary school and in the surrounding 'educative community' of legal and social welfare institutions. The tasks specified to undertake the project of making a self did not recognize relationships of interdependence as integral to that process. Indeed, these expectations formulated the ideal of the modern, autonomous personality as achieved through abandoning – throwing off – relationships of connectedness and the 'childish' emotional needs for such relationships. The spheres of human concern traditionally associated with the feminine – the world of the emotions, of intimacy and care – were to be left behind, negated, in the process of growing up. The gendered character of these assumptions about identity formation were obvious in debates about juvenile delinquency in the 1950s. Young men in this context, it seemed, were considered 'at risk' as they faced the burdens and pleasures of the freedom apparently only confronting their sex in the modern world. Only they need be – and were, so it was claimed – troubled by the requirement to make a self and life for themselves.

Nevertheless, in the setting of the secondary school, normative definitions of a 'proper growing up' insisted that both young men and young women were required to undertake the tasks said to be necessary to become a modern individual. These vocabularies circled around young women increasingly in the 1950s and 1960s seeking to speak of both the pleasures and obligations they should experience in the process of growing up. Educational reforms in this period, too, set out to ensure that the practices of the secondary school would train young women to understand themselves and their lives according to these cultural norms. Claiming the authority of science, these definitions of growing up assumed a neutral guise and decreed that all young people should evaluate themselves and their lives according to a set of judgements about their 'needs' as adolescents.

Notions of a 'proper growing up', then, whether in the popular culture contexts of mass-circulation newspapers and magazines or in the professional literature and practices of educational, legal and welfare institutions, translated the cultural ideal of the self-determining, autonomous individual into a set of normative definitions specifying how this status was to be attained. They counterposed the freedom said to be necessary to its achievement to what were claimed to be the needs of society. The period of youth gave young people time and space in which to make a self, free from the demands of society (though monitored and watched over by its agents); maturity meant the end of that freedom and the burden and risks of the project of making a self.

In the context of the modernized secondary school, however, young women would encounter alternative constructions of the self. Through the policies and practices of schools around such issues as the provision of domestic education for girls and the need for single-sex or co-educational schooling, all young women were increasingly identified in the 1950s and 1960s as, first and foremost, gendered beings. The apparent importance of 'achieving' an adult identity competed with claims that their sex predetermined who they were and would become. Yet, in marking out the terrain of the essential feminine, the secondary school of the 1950s was not entirely consistent. Domestic education, now increasingly considered a necessity for all young women, recruited the story of growing up as a modern individual to an account of young women making themselves ready for the roles of wife and mother. A female adult identity thus also required undertaking a series of tasks; it involved making a self. Adult womanhood, in this context, was an attainment rather than something young women necessarily became simply by virtue of their sex. By the same token, this feminine achievement story found its meaning and significance in the very clearly defined ending of taking on the roles of wife and mother. An open-ended project of making a self had no place – could not be contemplated – in this context.

In the educational rhetoric and policies instituted in the 1950s and early 1960s to provide domestic education for all girls, assumptions about the common destiny considered desirable for all members of their sex constituted the terms in which sex differences were to be understood in the modern secondary school. Debates about co-education, however, delineated the role of the secondary school as monitoring and shaping a sexualized being. Both sides of the debate, in this instance, agreed that sexual identities defined the terms in which sex differences should be recognized and managed by the secondary education system. In this version of the young woman's essential femininity, a (hetero)sexual identity held the supposed key to the pattern of her adolescence and maturity. Though the ending remained the same – she was still expected to 'choose' to become a wife and mother – her preoccupations during the time of her schooling were differently defined and organized by the practices of the secondary school that attempted to intervene in this aspect of her growing up. Co-education, its advocates claimed, monitored and assisted a sexualized identity to develop in the appropriate form. Single-sex education, according to its supporters, recognized that a sexualized identity already existed in the adolescent and would 'naturally' seek premature expression in the secondary school, but must be held in check for its proper enjoyment in adult life. The co-education debate and the tensions it created around the type of schools to be built in the rapidly expanding secondary education system of the 1950s and 1960s, constituted girls, relative newcomers to this institution, as a different and problematic sexualized presence.

While the secondary school became concerned with systematizing and augmenting sex differences in these various ways, the consumer culture increasingly defined a femininity absorbed in a presentation of body and self. Young women were urged to make and remake themselves in desirable form in the restless search for guarantees to ensure that they became the 'loved individuals' of the romance narrative. Yet, as I argued in Chapter 7, these claims about the significance of surfaces or image were also trainings in disengaging one's supposed essential self from one's femininity. Maturity in this context entailed an achievement of a body and personality under perfect control, closed off, ready to be viewed as object from every angle. Teenagerhood, however, allowed young women to experiment with taking on and off different types of femininity, a playing with those images. And, at times, young women totally disrupted all notions of femininity as object-to-be-looked-at by demanding a public visibility for themselves as femininity-out-of-control in the form of the teenage fan.

Surrounded by these competing definitions of her girlhood and growing up, the young woman of the 1950s and early 1960s could, nevertheless, be certain of a number of things. First, whether as 'youth', 'adolescent', 'teenager', 'teenage girl' or 'modern schoolgirl', she was being told that she was going through a particular stage in her life. As such, she had distinctive needs and interests that made her a member of a specific group, a separate category of person. Second, all these claims to define the nature of her concerns described her central preoccupation as focusing on the project of making a self, shaping an identity for herself – whether as an autonomous self or as some form of feminine self. Third, the young woman heard repeatedly that her happiness depended on the completion of that process. The excitement of youth, the period of adventure and experimentation, was to be relinquished for the security of belonging, of having a clearly defined identity and place in the social world. Finally, the competing definitions of girlhood and growing all shared the assumption that the young woman would find in herself both the need for the freedom to make a self and the desire to renounce that freedom in her attaining maturity. Young women clearly learnt the importance and significance of growing up. They were beset, however, by competing and not always consistent normative ideals of the tasks involved and how to effect a satisfactory closure of this process – of what it meant to be grown up.

The investigation carried out in this book of the increasing importance of normative definitions of growing up in shaping the experiences of young women in the 1950s and 1960s points to at least some of the reasons why many would find so powerful, the notions of an 'awakening of women' articulated by second-wave feminism in the following decades. Betty Friedan's call for women to grow up, to develop fully as individuals, offered a solution to the tensions produced by the antagonistic claims surrounding young women as they attempted to understand what was required of them in the process and completion of their growing up.

Friedan planted the cultural ideal of the self-determining individual at the heart of the aspirations of second-wave feminism in the 1960s and 1970s, but she neglected to interrogate the way in which that ideal had been formulated. In seeking to 'awaken women' from imposed, normative definitions of womanhood, she affirmed the tradition of constituting ideas and ideals of femaleness through a series of negations. She failed, too, to scrutinize the extent to which the ideal of the self-determining individual had increasingly in the twentieth century been translated into cultural norms which designated 'making a self', a project to be undertaken for only a specific period in a person's life and a project that should be completed, closed off, at the end of that time.

Recent feminist critiques of these norms of human growth and development, however, have undertaken this critique of the ideal of the self-determining individual. They claim, as I indicated in Chapter 1, that the form in which this ideal has been interpreted in normative accounts of growing up has enabled masculine norms and experiences of identity formation to acquire the status of universal prescriptions. Feminist writers like Carol Gilligan have sought public recognition and legitimacy for a different way of imagining the self – a relational self – which has arisen through, what these authors claim to be, women's different experience of growing up.

The alternative understanding of the project of feminism which has emerged from this analysis of women's different experiences has, however, established its own set of normative definitions of a 'proper growing up'. A certain way of being-in-the-world now becomes the goal of this process, as well as the source of its meaning and significance. In this conception of feminism, women find their strength and sense of belonging in recognizing or awakening to the possibilities of defining a different, autonomous 'truth of women' and a particular way of 'being-in-the-world' becomes itself a new normative description or goal of female subjectivity. Feminism in this guise is in danger of forfeiting its claim to be an on-going critique of the imposition of all normative definitions of womanhood. It becomes instead a project of the growing up of women that seeks a point of closure in which women can find a home, a sense of belonging, in the category 'woman' or in the orthodoxies of feminism itself. Such a project denies the diverse nature of the modern self, claiming that women are to look for the truth of themselves as encapsulated in the definition of their womanhood, and it recognizes community – the possibility of a shared life and struggle – only in sameness.

As Jeffrey Weeks notes, the increasing proliferation of social belongings and identities in the contemporary social world works to

undermine the possibility that any one of those forms of identification can successfully proclaim itself the truth of an individual.[2] The
search for community based on sameness is founded on denials and
exclusions in which many aspects of the individual self have to be
suppressed, at the same time as those who are different are shut out,
negated. The challenge of modernity, Weeks argues, is to refuse to
retreat into forms of community where identity becomes a fixed
attribute to be held onto at any cost.[3] The cultural ideal of the self-
determining, autonomous individual has constituted a major tradition in Western political and social thought concerned to grapple
with the possibilities and terrors for the modern individual of refusing to accept or retreat into fixed notions of identity. That ideal as
we have seen, however, has been conceptualized in such a way as
to become the means of the imposition of normative definitions of
subjectivity in a diverse range of settings rather than their refusal.
Feminism today needs, then, to contribute to the conceptualization
of forms of political community that recognize the diversity of
modern selves. Yet, at the same time, I am suggesting, it needs to
embrace the challenge which various formulations of the cultural
ideal of the self-determining individual have claimed to grasp but
have consistently failed to confront fully. Feminism today needs to
understand itself as an open-ended, on-going project of the critique
of prejudices and normative definitions of subjectivity, and of feminine subjectivity in particular. It needs to recognize the project of
'the growing up of women' as an open-ended one, a project for
which there can be no clear developmental path and no satisfactory
point of closure, no ending.
    What does such a commitment mean, however, in the life of the
individual? Minnie Bruce Pratt in her powerful narrative, 'Identity:
Skin Blood Heart', seeks to rethink the relationships between identity
and community. Her essay constitutes a major contribution to this
feminist project of reconceptualizing the forms of political collectivity.
I point to it here, however, as a very different account of a woman
growing up. As she describes her personal history, Pratt tells a story,
not of development or awakening, but of a constant and open-
ended expansion of the self. In this narrative, her childhood as a
white, middle-class gentile living in Alabama in the USA is not
something left behind, gone beyond, but something returned to at
different moments in her life, to be understood, re-evaluated, and
reintegrated anew into the self in a different form. As Biddy Martin
and Chandra Talpade Mohanty make clear in their detailed reading
of her text, there is no linear or developmental notion of the formation of identity in Pratt's account of her own history: 'The "self" in
this narrative is not an essence or truth concealed by patriarchal

Freida's interpretation

layers of deceit and lying in wait of discovery, revelation, or birth.'⁴
Minnie Bruce Pratt writes of a relational self, but hers is a diverse
self, shaped in relationships of power and dominance in which she
is implicated: relationships of connectedness where exclusions and
the negation of difference have also to be acknowledged as central.
Pratt tells a story of growing up that acknowledges the longing for
safe places, for a sense of belonging, a sense of a home; but she seeks
an understanding and an experience of such a place that is, in her
terms, not childish. In this narrative, no closure is possible on the
self; she seeks to live as, she says, 'on the edge of my skin',⁵ to be
involved in a constant expansion of the self. The sense of belonging
she pursues is to be provided by a place which enables such a project
of the self, a place too of mutuality, companionship and creativity,
yet a place that is inherently unstable, historically contingent and
unprotected.

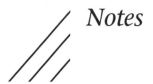

Notes

Preface

1 G. Greer, 'Greer at 50. On growing old but not growing up', *Vogue*, London, January 1989, pp. 101, 138.

Introduction

1 For example, S. Rowbotham, *Woman's Consciousness, Man's World*, Harmondsworth, Penguin, 1973, p. 5.
2 B. Friedan, *The Feminine Mystique*, Harmondsworth, Penguin, 1983, p. 70.
3 Friedan, p. 60.
4 M. Nava, 'Consumerism and its Contradictions', *Cultural Studies*, 1, 2, 1987, p. 204.
5 Second-wave feminism is the term commonly used to refer to the feminist movement which emerged in various Western countries in the late 1960s and early 1970s. See, for example, H. Eisenstein, *Contemporary Feminist Thought*, Sydney, Allen and Unwin, 1985.
6 See J. Habermas, 'Modernity – An Incomplete Project', in H. Foster (ed.), *Postmodern Culture*, London, Pluto Press, 1985. This notion will be explained and examined in Chapter 2.
7 For example, in the Australian context, the film 'For Love or Money' also represented the 1950s as largely significant for women in these same terms.
8 For example, H. Townsend, *The Baby Boomers, Growing up in Australia in the 1940s, 50s and 60s*, Brookvale, Simon Schuster, 1988.
9 See M. Foucault, *Language, Counter-Memory, Practice: Selected Essays and Interviews*, D.F. Bouchard (ed.), D.F. Bouchard and S. Simon (trans.), Oxford, Basil Blackwell, 1977.
10 J. Matthews, 'Feminist History', *Labour History*, No. 50, 1986, p. 150. Judith Allen has gone so far as to question whether feminist

historians should attempt to work within the discipline of history at all. She argues that notions of what counts as legitimate evidence and the modes of interpretation which continue to dominate in this discipline make it inevitable that only masculine versions of the past can be heard. See J. Allen, 'Evidence and Silence: Feminism and the limits of history', in C. Pateman and E. Gross (eds), *Feminist Challenges: Social and Political Theory*, Sydney, Allen and Unwin, 1986.

11 Matthews, p. 148.

12 D. Riley, *'Am I that Name?' Feminism and the category of 'Women' in History*, Minneapolis, University of Minnesota Press, 1988, p. 109.

13 Riley, p. 103.

14 J.W. Scott, *Gender and the Politics of History*, New York, Columbia University Press, 1988, p. 6. See also, C. Mohanty, 'Under Western Eyes: Feminist scholarship and colonial discourses', *Feminist Review*, 30, 1988.

15 Feminist History Group, 'Feminism as Femininity in the Nineteen Fifties?', *Feminist Review*, No. 3, 1979, p. 51.

16 A.M. Wolpe, 'The Official Ideology of Education for Girls', in M. Flude and J. Ahier (eds), *Educability, Schools and Ideology*, New York, John Wiley, 1974.

17 D. Thom, 'Better a Teacher than a Hairdresser? "A mad passion for equality" or keeping Molly and Betty down', in F. Hunt (ed.), *Lessons for Life: The Schooling of Girls and Women, 1850–1950*, London, Basil Blackwell, 1987, p. 134.

18 D. Thom, p. 131. Her assertion that gender differences can be seen with 'the naked eye' is obviously a highly problematic one about the 'naturalness' of gender differences, but this issue is not relevant to the specific focus of my discussion here, and hence I make no comment on it in my text.

19 C. Steedman, *The Tidy House: Little Girls Writing*, London, Virago, 1982, pp. 140–1.

20 In making these claims I am rejecting another fundamental assumption of much contemporary equal opportunity literature in the field of education that girls need female role models in areas such as science if they are to be persuaded to undertake these subjects.

21 I am not discounting here the points made by various feminist writers about the individual being a masculine figure (see Chapter 1), but I do wish to claim that the disembodiment of this figure, which she points to as necessary to disguise this masculinity, at the same time does leave open the very possibilities I discuss here. This issue is taken further in Chapters 4–7.

22 J. Ker Conway, *The Road to Coorain: An Australian Memoir*, London, Heinemann, 1989. Conway describes herself as having 'unthinkingly taken on the identity of the male writer and intellect' in her secondary and tertiary education. It is not until she misses out on a public service job because of her sex that she begins to identify herself as a 'woman' and to recognize the way in which her identification by society in these terms renders her intellect invisible. See Conway,

p. 171f. It is the possibility of this 'unthinkingness' that I wish to point to.

23 I further discuss this point about the different types of education provided for young women in this period and the class factors determining their access to education in Chapter 5.

24 Riley, p. 96.

25 T. de Lauretis, *Technologies of Gender: Essays on Theory, Film and Fiction*, Bloomington, Indiana University Press, 1989.

1 Feminism and the 'awakening of women'

1 *Age*, 14 February 1990, 'Tempo', p. 2.

2 S. Rowbotham, *The Past is Before Us: Feminism in Action since the 1960s*, London, Pandora, 1989, pp. xii, 295, 296.

3 Rowbotham, p. 298.

4 A. Oakley, *Taking it Like a Woman*, London, Fontana, 1985, pp. 57, 201.

5 C. Gilligan, 'Remapping the Moral Domain: New images of the self in relationship', in T. Heller *et al.* (eds), *Reconstructing Individualism: Autonomy, Individuality, and the Self in Western Thought*, Stanford, Calif., Stanford University Press, 1986, p. 250.

6 Gilligan, p. 251.

7 Gilligan, p. 249.

8 C. Gilligan, *In a Different Voice*, Cambridge, Mass., Harvard University Press, 1982, p. 173.

9 N. Chodorow, quoted in E. Abel *et al.* (eds), *The Voyage In: Fictions of Female Development*, Hanover, University Press of New England, 1983, p. 10.

10 Abel *et al.*

11 Friedan, p. 270.

12 S. Benhabib and D. Cornell (eds), Introduction to *Feminism as Critique*, Minneapolis, University of Minnesota Press, 1987, p. 1.

13 Gilligan, *In a Different Voice*, p. 174.

14 For a discussion of how Gilligan's work lends itself to such normative frameworks in equal opportunity strategies in education, see L. Johnson, 'Gender Issues and Education', *Australian Feminist Studies*, 11, 1990.

15 P. Adams and J. Minson, 'The "Subject" of Feminism', *M/F*, 2, 1978, p. 44.

16 Although these comments are more pertinent to Gilligan's followers than to her own book, her assumption in that work that there are only two types of subjectivities – the masculine and the feminine – leaves her open to this criticism. She does acknowledge that not all women take on the feminine self, or fit comfortably within it, but they are the exceptions. She speaks, however, of 'a different truth of women', thereby establishing a normative and ahistorical model of an authentic female self.

17 J. Henriques *et al.*, *Changing the Subject*, London, Methuen, 1984, p. 3.

18 J. Grumley, 'Two Views of the Paradigm of Production', *Praxis International*, 12/2, forthcoming 1992 (p. 13).
19 J. Minson, *Genealogies of Morals: Nietzsche, Foucault, Donzelot and the Eccentricity of Ethics*, London, Macmillan, 1985, p. 44.
20 M. Foucault, 'Technologies of the Self', in L.H. Martin (ed.), *Technologies of the Self: A Seminar with Michel Foucault*, London, Tavistock Publications, 1988, p. 18.
21 Foucault, 'Technologies of the Self'.
22 C. Pateman, 'The Concept of Equity', in P.N. Troy (ed.), *A Just Society? Essays on Equity in Australia*, Sydney, Allen and Unwin, 1981, p. 35.
23 S. Benhabib, 'The Generalized and the Concrete Other: The Kohlberg–Gilligan controversy in feminist theory', in S. Benhabib and D. Cornell (eds), *Feminism as Critique: On the Politics of Gender*, Minneapolis, University of Minnesota Press, 1987, p. 85.
24 See M. Markus, 'Women, Success and Civil Society: Submission to, or subversion of, the Achievement Principle', in Benhabib and Cornell (eds), 1987.
25 P. Johnson, 'Quest for the Self: Feminism's appropriation of Romanticism', unpublished paper delivered at the Department of General Philosophy Seminar, University of Sydney, April 1992.
26 See R. Felski, *Beyond Feminist Aesthetics*, London, Hutchinson Radius, 1989, p. 78.
27 See E. Grosz, *Jacques Lacan: A Feminist Introduction*, Sydney, Allen and Unwin, 1990, p. 8.
28 Riley, pp. 3–4.
29 M. Morris,'Things to do with Shopping Centres', in S. Sheridan (ed.), *Grafts: Feminist Cultural Criticism*, London, Verso, 1988, p. 194.
30 M. Foucault, *Politics, Philosophy, Culture: Interviews and Other Writings, 1977–1984*, L.D. Kritzman (ed.), New York, Routledge, 1988, p. 119.
31 B. Martin and C.T. Mohanty, 'Feminist Politics: What's home got to do with it?', in T. de Lauretis, *Feminist Studies/Critical Studies*, London, Macmillan, 1988.

2   The importance of having

1 D. Frisby, *Fragments of Modernity: Theories of Modernity in the Work of Simmel, Kracauer and Benjamin*, Cambridge, Polity Press, 1985, p. 2.
2 M. Berman, *All that is Solid Melts into Air*, London, Verso, 1985.
3 Berman, p. 345.
4 Berman, p. 16.
5 Berman, p. 16.
6 Berman, p. 85.
7 Berman, pp. 345–6.
8 Berman, p. 98.
9 Berman, p. 74.
10 Morris, p. 202.

11 F. Moretti, *The Way of the World: The* Bildungsroman *in European Culture*, London, Verso, 1987, p. 174.
12 A. Huyssen, 'Mass Culture as Woman: Modernism's Other', in T. Modleski (ed.), *Studies in Entertainment: Critical Approaches to Mass Culture*, Bloomington, Indiana University Press, 1986, p. 196.
13 Huyssen, p. 204.
14 Nava, p. 208.
15 J. Donzelot, *The Policing of Families*, R. Hurley (trans.), New York, Pantheon Books, 1979. For a useful discussion of Donzelot's argument and the type of feminist analysis it challenges, see J. Minson, *Genealogies of Morals: Nietzsche, Foucault, Donzelot, and the Eccentricity of Ethics*, London, Macmillan, 1985.
16 Nava, p. 206.
17 Nava, p. 206, and see also p. 207.
18 Nava, p. 207. Nava continues to avoid specifying precisely what she means by 'agency' in her more recent paper on consumerism. She simply asserts that it is a 'good thing' to recognize agency. Yet such a stance would appear to rely on the humanist framework which Foucault rejects. See M. Nava, 'Consumerism Reconsidered: Buying and power', *Cultural Studies*, 5, 2, 1991, p. 165.
19 These studies of post-Second World War youth will be looked at in greater detail in the following chapter. See S. Hall and T. Jefferson (eds), *Resistance through Rituals*, London, Hutchinson, 1976.
20 J. Radway, *Reading the Romance: Women, Patriarchy, and Popular Literature*, Chapel Hill, University of North Carolina Press, 1984.
21 J. Fiske, 'Women and Quiz Shows: Consumerism, patriarchy and resisting pleasures', in M.E. Brown (ed.), *Television and Women's Culture: The Politics of the Popular*, Sydney, Currency Press, 1989, p. 142.
22 M. E. Brown, 'Consumption and Resistance – The problem of pleasure', in Brown, p. 210.
23 J. Williamson, 'The Problems of Being Popular', *New Socialist*, 41, September 1986, pp. 14–16. Mica Nava also refers to this article by Williamson.
24 P. Petro, 'Modernity and Mass Culture in Weimar: Contours of a discourse on sexuality in early theories of perception and representation', *New German Critique*, 40, 1987. See also her *Joyless Streets: Women and Melodramatic Representation in Weimar Germany*, Princeton, Princeton University Press, 1989.

3 Growing up as a modern individual

1 Moretti, p. 185.
2 Moretti, p. 15.
3 Moretti, p. 16.
4 Moretti, p. 7.
5 Moretti, p. 65.
6 Moretti, p. 5.

7 Moretti, p. 174. See also Chapter 2 for a further exploration of this aspect of Moretti's argument.
8 See Chapter 2.
9 J. Clarke *et al.*, 'Subcultures, Cultures and Class: A theoretical overview', in S. Hall and T. Jefferson (eds), *Resistance through Rituals*, London, Hutchinson, 1976, p. 9.
10 See Richard Hoggart, *The Uses of Literacy*, London, Chatto and Windus, 1957.
11 S. Hall, 'The Emergence of Cultural Studies and the Crisis of the Humanities', *October*, 53, 1990, p. 12.
12 Moretti, p. 185.
13 D. Riesman, *The Lonely Crowd: A Study of the Changing American Character*, New Haven, Yale University Press, (1950) 1969, p. 22.
14 Riesman, p. xxx.
15 Riesman, pp. 48–9.
16 Riesman, pp. xiv, 21–2.
17 Riesman, p. 44.
18 As Riesman notes in his 1969 preface, this ideal was not clearly spelt out in his concluding chapter; see pp. xix–xx.
19 W. Breines, 'The 1950s: Gender and some social science', *Sociological Inquiry*, 56, 1, 1986, p. 75.
20 As I note below, Riesman did indicate some awareness of changes occurring in the way in which young women were making the transition to adulthood in the years after the war. See Riesman, pp. 41–2.
21 I take this term from the work of P. Cohen, 'Rethinking the Youth Question', *Working Paper*, 3, Post-16 Education Centre, in association with Youth and Policy, London Institute of Education, 1986.
22 P. Goodman, *Growing Up Absurd: Problems of Youth in the Organized System*, London, Victor Gollancz, 1961, p. 13.
23 Apart from Riesman's and Goodman's writings and that of R.J. Havighurst examined in the following chapter, I am referring here to studies such as: E.Z. Friedenburg, *The Vanishing Adolescent*, Boston, Beacon Press, 1959; D. Ausubel, *Theory and Problems of Adolescent Development*, New York, Grune and Stratton, 1954; and J. Coleman, *The Adolescent Society*, New York, Free Press of Glencoe, 1961.
24 Moretti, pp. 8–9.

4 Growing up in modern Australia

1 See M. Schudson, quoted by G. Whitwell, *Making the Market: The Rise of the Consumer Society*, Melbourne, McPhee Gribble, 1989, p. 10.
2 *Age*, 12 September 1955, p. 5.
3 *Age*, 1 January 1951, p. 2.
4 *Age*, 29 December 1954, p. 2; 12 May 1954, p. 2; *Sydney Morning Herald* (SMH), 22 April 1955, Supplement, pp. 4, 9.
5 *SMH*, 7 November 1961, p. 7.
6 See p. 117f.
7 In 1947, 15.3 per cent of women in paid employment were married;

by 1961, this proportion had jumped to 38.3 per cent. This change needs to be understood in the context of the greater rate of increase in the female workforce compared to the male workforce in this period, but also of the growing number of migrant women joining the workforce.

8 Before the Second World War, the majority of home owners owned the houses they lived in outright. After the war, the percentage of households recorded as in the process of purchasing their homes – i.e. through loan schemes – increased from 7.9 per cent in 1947 to 15.1 per cent in 1954 and to 22.5 per cent in 1961. See Whitwell, p. 36. By 1961, 71 per cent of Sydney's private dwellings were owner-occupied. See P. Spearritt, *Sydney Since the Twenties*, Sydney, Hale and Iremonger, 1978, p. 105.

9 Whitwell, p. 26.

10 D. Horne, *The Lucky Country*, Harmondsworth, Penguin, (1964) 1971, pp. 18, 21.

11 In more recent work, Horne has commented on the extent to which this irony was misunderstood; the phrase 'the lucky country' was taken up in various settings in the late 1960s to feed the very complacency he had set out to disrupt. See D. Horne, *The Lucky Country Revisited*, Melbourne, Dent, 1987.

12 Horne, *The Lucky Country Revisited*, pp. 76–80.

13 S. Lees and J. Senyard, *The 1950s. . . . How Australia became a Modern Society, and Everyone got a House and a Car*, Melbourne, Hyland House, 1987, p. 72.

14 M. Pumphrey, 'The Flapper, the Housewife and the Making of Modernity', *Cultural Studies*, 1, 2, 1987, p. 185.

15 See, for example, O.A. Oeser (ed.), *Teacher, Pupil, and Task: Elements of Social Psychology Applied to Education*, London, Tavistock Publications, (1955) 1960, p. xii.

16 K.S. Cunningham (ed.), *The Adjustment of Youth: A Study of a Social Problem in the British, American, and Australian Communities*, Melbourne, Melbourne University Press, 1951, p. v.

17 Cunningham, p. 1.

18 Cunningham, p. 5. For a further example of a text which was both constituting a number of fields of enquiry about 'the social adjustment' of young people in the Australian context and setting out the arguments for the academic legitimacy of these fields and their political importance, see O.A. Oeser and S.B. Hammond (eds), *Social Structure and Personality in a City*, London, Routledge and Kegan Paul, 1954.

19 Cunningham, p. 241.

20 W.F. Connell *et al.*, *Growing Up in an Australian City: A Study of Adolescents in Sydney*, Melbourne, Australian Council of Educational Research (ACER), 1959, pp. 8, 204.

21 Connell *et al.*, pp. 207–10.

22 See, for example, N.M. Oddie and D. Spearitt, *Some Activities of Australian Adolescents*, Vols I and II, Melbourne, ACER, 1958; W.J.

Campbell, *Television – and the Australian Adolescent*, Sydney, Angus and Robertson, 1962.

23 M. Finnane, 'Censorship and the Child: Explaining the comics campaign', *Australian Historical Studies*, 23, 92, 1989.

24 P. Cole (ed.), *The Education of the Adolescent in Australia*, Melbourne, ACER, 1935, pp. xi–xii.

25 K.S. Cunningham, 'Admission Requirements, Tests and Examinations', in Cole (ed.), p. 258.

26 R. Teese, 'The Evolution of the Victorian Secondary School System', in L. Johnson and D. Tyler (eds), *Cultural Politics: Papers in Contemporary Australian Education, Culture and Politics*, Melbourne Working Papers, Vol. 5, 1984, p. 126ff.

27 W.F. Connell, 'Trends in Educational Research Since World War Two', Presidential Address to the Australian Association for Educational Research, 1973, W.F. Connell Papers, University of Sydney Archives. For an example of how education was discussed in these terms during the war, see 'Interim Report of Council to Minister of Public Instruction: Educational Reform', The Council of Public Education (Victoria), 33rd Annual Report, 1943.

28 *Report of the Committee Appointed to Survey Secondary Education in New South Wales* (Wyndham Report), 1957, p. 11.

29 Wyndham Report, p. 16.

30 Wyndham Report, pp. 63, 87.

31 Wyndham Report, pp. 67, 85.

32 For example, at the University of Melbourne, his work appeared as a key text on the reading list of the first-year course of the Bachelor of Education (the teacher training course) from 1957.

33 R.J. Havighurst, *Human Development and Education*, New York, Longmans, Green and Co, (1953) 1955, p. 159.

34 Havighurst, p. 332.

35 Havighurst, p. 5.

36 Havighurst, p. 22.

37 Havighurst, p. 120.

38 For an important discussion of popular education, particularly the elementary school, in these terms, see I. Hunter, *Culture and Government: The Emergence of Literary Education*, London, Macmillan, 1988.

39 Havighurst, p. 2. As will be shown in Chapter 6, bringing the peer culture into the school did not necessarily ensure that this space became one in which young people could be successfully supervised.

40 For a further discussion of developmental psychology, see V. Walkerdine, 'Developmental Psychology and the Child-centred Pedagogy: The insertion of Piaget into early education', in Henriques *et al.*, p. 154.

41 Abel *et al.*, pp. 10–11.

42 Connell *et al.*, p. 203.

43 Connell *et al.*, p. 203.

44 Havighurst, p. 116.

45 N. Rose, 'Psychology as a "Social" Science' in I. Parker and J. Shotter

(eds), *Deconstructing Social Psychology*, London, Routledge, 1990, p. 108.
46 See Chapter 1.

5 The modern school girl

1 *Age*, 3 May 1952, p. 7.
2 A.A. Phillips, 'The Schools', in P. Coleman (ed.), *Australian Civilization*, Melbourne, F.W. Cheshire, 1962, p. 108.
3 B.K. Hyams and B. Bessant, *Schools for the People?*, Hawthorn, Longman, 1972; A. Barcan, 'The Transition in Australian Education 1939-67', in J. Cleverley and J. Lawry (eds), *Australian Education in the Twentieth Century*, Hawthorn, Longman, 1972; *Age*, 7 November 1962, p. 10 and 17 December 1959, p. 2. Catholic schools were unable to cope with the increase of pupils at the primary and secondary levels and, by the early 1960s, this crisis itself was to begin to have its own specific political effects.
4 ACER, *The Shire of Ferntree Gully and its Educational Future*, Melbourne, ACER, 1956, pp. 44-5.
5 A.G.T. Zainuddin, *They Dreamt of a School: A Centenary History of Methodist Ladies College Kew 1882-1982*, Melbourne, Hyland House, 1982, pp. 259-60.
6 *Report of the Committee on State Education in Victoria* (Ramsay Report), 1960, p. 102.
7 Wyndham Report, pp. 56-7.
8 See Chapter 3.
9 Wyndham Report, p. 60.
10 Wyndham Report, pp. 57-61.
11 Hunter, p. 123.
12 *Age*, 21 September 1950, p. 9.
13 *SMH*, Schools Supplement, 14 January 1954, p. 1.
14 *Age*, Literary Section, 12 May 1951, p. 4.
15 See, for example, *Age*, 17 August 1956, p. 2; 20 September 1956, p. 2.
16 *SMH*, 11 October 1957, p. 8.
17 Wyndham Report, p. 82.
18 *Age*, 2 February 1960, p. 5. For a detailed discussion of this fund, see D. Smart, 'The Industrial Fund: A highly successful model of big business collaboration with the Headmasters' Conference in the interests of school science', in I. Palmer (ed.), *Melbourne Studies in Education*, Melbourne, Melbourne University Press, 1984.
19 This initiative was controversial as it broke with the tradition of no state funding for private schools established in Australia in the late nineteenth century. For a detailed discussion of this move and, in particular, of this aspect of its significance, see P.N. Gill, 'The Federal Science Grant: An episode in church and state relations, 1963-1964', in E.L. French (ed.), *Melbourne Studies in Education*, Melbourne, Melbourne University Press, 1964.

20 I. Clunies-Ross, 'The Dilemma of Modern Education', *The Journal of Education*, 3, 3, 1956, p. 102.
21 *Sun-Herald*, 24 January 1960, p. 95.
22 *Age*, 5 October 1953, p. 3; 13 October 1956, p. 2; 6 June 1957, p. 12; 19 November 1957, p. 5.
23 *SMH*, 10 January 1958, p. 2.
24 Submissions and Exhibits, 1954–55, Survey of Secondary Education Committee, 10/31658, E15, New South Wales State Archives.
25 N. Mackenzie, *Women in Australia*, Melbourne, F.W. Cheshire, 1962, p.102. For one of the early documents pushing for greater equality of education opportunities for girls, see the publication of the Victorian Secondary Teachers' Association, *The Secondary Teacher*, 102, February 1965.
26 *SMH*, 26 November 1953, 'Women's Section', p. 7. Similar stories appeared in this paper each year at about the same time.
27 *Cinesound Review*, issue no. 1131, 3 July 1953, National Sound Archives, Canberra.
28 Ramsay Report, p. 35.
29 J. Newsom, *The Education of Girls*, London, Faber and Faber, 1948, p. 12.
30 Newsom, p. 24. Newsom's list reads much like the claims made in a women's liberation poster of the 1970s advertising the job of a housewife which listed the many qualities and skills required.
31 Minson, p. 208f.
32 See Chapters 1 and 2 for a detailed development of this argument.
33 These were practices pointed to by the first major report on the experience of education for young women produced in Australia, the *Girls, Schools and Society* report published by the Commonwealth Schools Commission, Canberra, AGPS, 1975.
34 *SMH*, 21 November 1957, p. 8.
35 'Views on Co-Education of the Staff of Sutherland Intermediate High School', July 1955, *Survey of Secondary Education*, New South Wales State Archives, 10/31663, E109.
36 *SMH*, 12 October 1954, p. 7; 13 May 1954, p. 2; 17 June 1955, p. 6.
37 *SMH*, 20 May 1954, p. 2.
38 Transcript of evidence from Headmasters' Association, p. 323, *Survey of Secondary Education*, New South Wales State Archives, 10/31658, E17.
39 *SMH*, 19 August 1961, p. 3.
40 *SMH*, 20 September 1961, p. 2.
41 *SMH*, 7 October 1954, p. 2.

6 Youth on the streets

1 See A.P. Jephcott, *Girls Growing Up*, London, Faber and Faber, 1942, p. 36.
2 M. Abrams, *The Teenage Consumer*, London, The London Press Exchange Ltd, 1959, p. 9.

3 Abrams, p. 10.
4 *SMH*, 14 November 1957, 'Women's Section', p. 4.
5 *Broadcasting and Television*, 4 October 1957, pp. 24–5.
6 *Broadcasting and Television*, 13 December 1957, p. 10.
7 These issues about the construction of young women as consumers will be looked at further in the following chapter.
8 S. Ewen, *Captains of Consciousness: Advertising and the Social Roots of the Consumer Culture*, New York, McGraw Hill, 1976, p. 137.
9 J.A. Blackmore, 'Schooling for Work: Vocationalism in secondary education in Victoria', PhD thesis, Stanford University, 1986, pp. 10–20.
10 *Sun-Herald*, 2 June 1957, p. 80.
11 *Age*, 19 December 1956, p. 2.
12 See Chapter 5.
13 These and following observations are based on readings of the following newspapers and magazines: the *Age*, *SMH*, *Sun-Herald*, the *Australian Women's Weekly*, the *New Idea*, the *Listener In* (which later becomes the *Listener In – TV*), *Rydge's* and *Broadcasting and Television*. The term 'teenager' was often in inverted commas in the early 1950s, and some uncertainty existed about whether the term should be hyphenated or not.
14 *Age*, 15 May 1954, p. 8.
15 *Age*, 14 May 1955, p. 17.
16 *Age*, 14 May 1955, p. 17.
17 See Chapter 3.
18 See, for example, *New Idea*, 26 August 1964, pp. 12–13, 47; and books such as *How to Live with Your Teen-ager*, by Dr Dorothy W. Baruch, New York, McGraw-Hill, 1953. See also Chapter 4.
19 See M. Finnane, 'Censorship and the Child: Explaining the comics campaign', *Australian Historical Studies*, 23, 92, 1989.
20 See, for example, *Age*, 11 November 1964, p. 14.
21 For a discussion of youth policy and debates about juvenile delinquency in a number of Australian states, see R. White and B. Wilson (eds), *For Your Own Good: Young People and State Intervention in Australia*, Special Issue of *Journal of Australian Studies*, 1991.
22 In the following account of the Barry Committee, I have drawn on an unpublished paper by Helen Bannister, 'Young, Male and Delinquent: A juvenile delinquency panic in Victoria 1956'.
23 Justice Barry, Chair of the Committee, *Report of Juvenile Delinquency Advisory Committee*, report to Hon. Rylah, MLA, Chief Secretary of Victoria, 17 July 1956 (Barry Report), p. 8.
24 Barry Report, p. 21.
25 Barry Report, p. 26.
26 Barry Report, p. 27.
27 As indicated below, the bodgie was a young person who wore clothes and hairstyles influenced by American seamen during the Second World War. Their fashions were said to have changed during the 1950s.

28 S. Cohen, *Folk Devils and Moral Panics: The Creation of the Mods and Rockers*, London, MacGibbon and Kee, 1972.
29 *Sun*, 5 April 1955, 6 April 1955 (quoted in Bannister, p. 12).
30 *Age*, 28 October 1955, p. 5.
31 *Age*, 14 October 1955, p. 5; 10 November 1955, p. 2; 7 December 1955, p. 8.
32 J.S. McDonald, 'The Bodgies: The socio-cultural effects of the impingement of American culture and society on Sydney, Australia, during World War II', B.A. honours thesis, University of Sydney, 1951, Section 21, pp. 1–2; see also, *SMH*, 21 January 1956, p. 2.
33 A.E. Manning, *The Bodgie: A Study in Psychological Abnormality*, Sydney, Angus and Robertson, 1958, p. 7.
34 Manning, pp. 89–90.
35 *SMH*, 21 January 1956, p. 2. Audrey Hepburn's film, 'Roman Holiday' with Cary Grant, had gained great popularity at this time.
36 *Age*, 10 January 1959, p. 18.
37 Bannister, p. 16.
38 See C. Dyhouse, *Girls Growing Up in Late Victorian and Edwardian England*, London, Routledge and Kegan Paul, 1981, p. 117.
39 Bannister, p. 27.
40 *Age*, 25 August 1954, p. 1. The girls were Pauline Parker, aged 16, and Juliet Hulme, aged 15, and they were accused of battering Pauline Parker's mother to death.
41 *Age*, 27 August 1954, p. 5. This royal tour is discussed further in Chapter 7.
42 *Sun-Herald*, 24 August 1954, p. 2.
43 *Sun-Herald*, 29 August 1954, p. 29. This article described how a 'normal' friendship between these girls gradually deteriorated until they were totally consumed with each other and the fantasy world 'of their own' they had created. The girls were declared sane and sentenced to be detained in prison 'during Her Majesty's pleasure', *Sun-Herald*, 29 August 1954, p. 1.
44 *Age*, 4 September 1952, p. 4.
45 *Age*, 1 October 1952, p. 4; 2 October 1952, p. 2. A newspaper report in 1960, with the headline 'Where girls learn the meaning of "home"', spoke in glowing terms of a new home and hostel for girls which suggested that the state was now taking its parental role seriously. Both were described as 'homely' and 'modern'; girls were provided with spaces of supervised freedom to allow them to learn to go back eventually to the 'ordinary' life of the community'. *Age*, 17 May 1960, p. 11.
46 *Age*, 9 December 1960, pp. 2, 5.
47 *Age*, 9 December 1960, p. 11.
48 *Age*, 9 December 1960, p. 2.
49 *Age*, 3 May 1958, p. 2.
50 *Age*, 5 May 1951, p. 2.
51 For a brief history of these organizations in Australia, see David Maunders, *Keeping them off the Streets*, Melbourne, Phillip Institute of Technology, 1984.

52 D.W. Hood, 'A Critical Evaluation of Youth Education in Australia', typewritten manuscript, dated 1952, held at the University of Melbourne, Education Library, p. 13.
53 Hood, pp. 50–1.
54 See Maunders, p. 92f.
55 *SMH*, 5 September 1957, p. 5.
56 See, for instance, the comments by the Reverend Alan Walker in the *SMH*, 5 May 1958, p. 5.
57 *SMH*, 21 April 1959, p. 9.
58 *Sun-Herald*, 10 August 1958, p. 15.
59 *Sun-Herald*, 29 March 1953, p. 15.
60 *Sun-Herald*, 6 January 1957, p. 31.
61 *Age*, 19 October 1959, p. 5.
62 *Age*, 15 June 1964, p. 1.
63 Barbara Ehrenreich *et al.*, 'Beatlemania: Girls just want to have fun', in *Remaking Love: The Feminization of Sex*, London, Fontana, 1986, p. 11.
64 Ehrenreich, p. 18.
65 Ehrenreich, pp. 17–18.
66 *Age*, 13 June 1964, p. 38.
67 *Age*, 3 May 1965, p. 11.
68 *SMH*, 3 July 1956, p. 1.
69 R. Gerster and J. Bassett, *Seizures of Youth: The Sixties and Australia*, Melbourne, Hyland House, 1991, p. 40.
70 *Age*, 1 April 1960, p. 5; see also, *Age*, 31 March 1960, p. 3.
71 *Age*, 28 May 1960, p. 8.
72 *Age*, 23 November 1961, p. 3; and see Gerster and Bassett, p. 37.
73 *SMH*, 19 February 1965, p. 2; see also 23 February 1965, p. 2.
74 *Age*, 23 October 1965, p. 1.
75 See, for example, *Age*, 10 February 1960, p. 14.

7 'The best of everything'

1 The film 'The Best of Everything' (based on the book by Rona Jaffe) was produced by Gerry Wald, starred Joan Crawford and was released by Twentieth Century Fox in 1959.
2 See M.A. Doane, *The Desire to Desire: The Woman's Film of the 1940s*, Bloomington, Indiana University Press, 1987; and D. Riley, *War in the Nursery: Theories of the Child and Mother*, London, Virago, 1983.
3 R.W. Connell, *Gender and Power*, Sydney, Allen and Unwin, 1987, p. 248.
4 *Sun-Herald*, 15 November 1964, p. 93.
5 H. Lefebvre, *Everyday Life in the Modern World*, Sacha Rabinovitch (trans.), New York, Harper Torchbooks, 1971, pp. 58, 73.
6 F. Jameson, 'Postmodernism and Consumer Society', in Foster, pp. 24–5.
7 Nava, 'Consumerism Reconsidered', p. 161.
8 See, for instance, Ewen, 1976, and Pumphrey, pp. 179–94.

9 See, for example, the following advertisements and feature articles: *SMH*, 10 July 1961, Australia Unlimited Supplement; *Sun-Herald*, 25 September 1955, p. 53 and 2 April 1961, p. 16; *Age*, 20 January 1960, p. 17 and 3 October 1960, p. 2.

10 *Age*, 20 January 1960, p. 17.

11 L. Mulvey, 'A Phantasmagoria of the Female Body: The work of Cindy Sherman', *New Left Review*, 188, 1991, pp. 148–9.

12 *SMH*, 21 January 1951, p. 14.

13 For example, *Teenage, Teenage Topics* and *Teenage and Women's Wear*.

14 These were the names used by Mark Foys in Sydney, Farmers and Co. in Sydney and Georges in Melbourne. See, for example, *Age*, 15 May 1954, p. 8.

15 Mary Ann Doane quotes Michael Renov as making the point that the consumer society after the Second World War claimed to delineate not only the duties but the desires of 'woman'. See Doane, p. 33.

16 See 'Cosmetics – The fragrant jungle', *Current Affairs Bulletin*, 25, 5, University of Sydney, 1960. This report refers to the increasing use of cosmetics by teenage girls in the 1950s.

17 A Berlei advertisement: *Age*, 7 March 1962, p. 12.

18 See J. Pearson and G. Turner, *The Persuasion Industry*, London, Eyre and Spottiswoode, 1965, which describes, for example, a campaign in 1960 for a new deodorant soap which targeted the female market in new ways. The authors claim that the success of this campaign's use of a glamorous model demonstrated that 'women of any class will identify themselves with a model *provided* she is beautiful enough'. They claim that the industry had previously assumed that such advertising would alienate 'hard-working housewives', but this campaign was 'appealing to something quite new in female advertising – to women's narcissism and their feelings about their own bodies' (p. 112).

19 *Age*, 20 August 1958, p. 11.

20 *Age*, 1 May 1958, p. 4.

21 See Holeproof advertisements for these stockings as giving 'Your legs an alive youthful look: Flaming Youth': *Age*, 26 July 1958, p. 8.

22 *Age*, 14 May 1959, p. 9.

23 See Chapter 6, pp. 92–5.

24 *New Idea*, 27 January 1965, p. 5.

25 *Sun-Herald*, 9 May 1965, p. 80.

26 *Sun-Herald*, 5 July 1964, p. 85; *Age*, 4 February 1965, p. 14; *Australian Women's Weekly*, 2 March 1960, pp. 8–9.

27 *New Idea*, 12 August 1953, p. 16.

28 *Age*, 10 December 1958, p. 10.

29 See A. Heller, 'The Dissatisfied Society', *Praxis International*, 2, 1982/3.

30 See Chapter 2, p. 30.

31 J. Winship, 'Woman Becomes an "Individual" – Femininity and consumption in women's magazines, 1954–69', Centre for

Contemporary Cultural Studies, Stencilled Occasional Paper, February 1981, p. 2.

32 *Australian Women's Weekly*, 30 September 1959, p. 4.
33 *Age*, 8 March 1950, p. 2; *Sun-Herald*, 14 February 1965, p. 5.
34 *New Idea*, 12 February 1964, p. 21.
35 *Australian Women's Weekly*, 2 September 1959, p. 11.
36 *Teen Twenty*, Summer Issue, 1964, p. 6.
37 *SMH*, 9 August 1956, p. 9.
38 *SMH*, 16 November 1957, p. 11.
39 *New Idea*, 12 February 1964, p. 21.
40 *Australian Women's Weekly*, 7 September 1960, p. 6; *Age*, 25 January 1963, p. 16; see also, *Myer News*, April 1958, p. 6; *New Idea*, 27 January 1965, pp. 14–15.
41 C. Pateman, quoted in N. Fraser, 'What's Critical about Critical Theory? The case of Habermas and gender', *New German Critique*, 35, 1985, p. 113.
42 *SMH*, 9 April 1964, p. 2; for the campaigns discussed here see, for example, *Age*, 30 August 1957, p. 5 and 3 November 1962, p. 3.
43 I.M. Young, 'Throwing like a Girl: A phenomenology of feminine body comportment, motility and spatiality', in J. Allen and I.M. Young (eds), *The Thinking Muse: Feminism and Modern French Philosophy*, Bloomington, Indiana University Press, 1989, pp. 65–6.
44 Young, p. 66.
45 Young, p. 67.
46 Young, p. 66.
47 I am arguing here that there were marked differences in the forms of bodily training received, for instance, by women of the upper classes, middle classes, domestic servant class and the working class in Australia at the beginning of the twentieth century.
48 Young, pp. 52–3.
49 Young, p. 65.
50 See J. Williamson, 'Images of "Woman" – The photographs of Cindy Sherman', *Screen*, 24, 6, 1983.
51 S. de Beauvoir, *Brigitte Bardot and the Lolita Syndrome*, New York, Arno Press and New York Times, 1972, p. 20.
52 *Age*, 21 January 1961, p. 19.
53 *Sun-Herald*, 30 September 1956, p. 17.
54 Doane, p. 182.
55 See M. Russo, 'Female Grotesques: Carnival and theory', in T. de Lauretis (ed.), *Feminist Studies/Critical Studies*, London, Macmillan, 1988, p. 224.
56 M. Bakhtin, *Rabelais and his World*, Bloomington, Indiana University Press, 1984.
57 For example, *Sun-Herald*, 28 September 1958, p. 53.
58 Russo, p. 218.
59 The YMCA and YWCA sponsored such publications, as did, for example, the Seventh Day Adventists and the Father and Son Welfare Movement. See, for example, *A Guide to Womanhood*, Sydney, Father

172   *The modern girl*

and Son Welfare Movement, 1960/62; *The Guide to 'Teen Years'*, Sydney, Father and Son Welfare Movement, 1959; H. Shyrock, *On Becoming a Woman*, Warburton, Victoria, Signs Publishing Company, ND; E. Millis Duvall, *The Art of Dating*, New York, Permabooks, 1958/ 60 (copyright on this publication was held by the YWCA).

60 H. Gurley Brown, *Sex and the Single Girl*, London, Frederick Muller Ltd, 1963.

61 *New Idea*, 10 April 1957, p. 34.

62 *New Idea*, 1 May 1961, p. 46.

63 *Sun-Herald*, 3 May 1959, p. 25. Although there was a range of groups involved in lobbying for these changes, my concern here is only with the way it was reported in the press and women's magazines as a story of the 'problem of the child bride evil'.

64 *Age*, 4 March 1954, p. 7. Considerable dismay was expressed in the Australian media when the Queen, in the interests of a democratic monarchy, announced in 1957 that there would be no more debutante balls at the palace. But balls in local and city town halls continued to flourish in Australia.

65 *Age*, 18 December 1950, p. 1.

66 *Age*, 20 April 1950, p. 2.

67 *Age*, 20 April 1950, p. 2.

68 *Age*, 4 October 1950, p. 2.

69 *Sun-Herald*, 2 September 1962, p. 110.

70 *Sun-Herald*, 17 March 1963, p. 5.

71 Australia, House of Representatives, 1962, *Debates*, Vol. 34, p. 213; see also Vol. 36, p. 1068 and Vol. 37, p. 2915.

72 According to Greg Whitwell, between 1947 and 1961, the labour force increased from 3.2 million to 4.23 million and about 73 per cent of this increase was due to immigrants arriving between these dates: Whitwell, p. 21; see also G. Bolton, *The Middle Way: The Oxford History of Australia, Vol. 5, 1942–1988*, Melbourne, Oxford University Press, 1990, pp. 53–7, 105–6.

73 *Age*, 31 July 1950, p. 3; 3 September 1955, p. 3.

74 *Age*, 9 January 1950, p. 5; 28 April 1950, p. 1.

75 The Queen occupied the front (and other) pages of the daily press and women's magazines in Australia throughout the period of her tour. A speech by the Governor of Victoria, Sir Dallas Brooks, provides one clear example of this notion of a romance between the Queen and the Australian people, as symbolized by its youth and their supposed sense of connectedness and similarity to her: *Age*, 3 February 1954, p. 3.

76 *Age*, 27 April 1959, p. 1.

77 *Age*, 16 November 1956, p. 8.

78 *Age*, 27 November 1956, pp. 1–2.

79 *Age*, 10 October 1950, p. 10.

80 *Age*, 3 October 1950, p. 6.

81 *Age*, 2 April 1951, p. 3.

82 *Age*, 10 November 1950, p. 3; see also *SMH*, 27 July 1951, p. 5.

83 *Age*, 2 January 1958, p. 8.
84 *SMH*, 1 July 1958, p. 5; 9 January 1959, p. 3.
85 *Age*, 16 December 1958, p. 6.
86 *Age*, 20 February 1959, p. 3.

Endings

1 *Australian Women's Weekly*, Teenagers' Weekly supplement, 22 February 1961, p. 5.
2 J. Weeks, 'Invented Moralities', *History Workshop*, 32, 1991, p. 155.
3 Weeks, p. 55.
4 Martin and Mohanty, p. 197.
5 M.N. Pratt, 'Identity: Skin Blood Heart', in E. Bulkin *et al.*, *Yours in Struggle: Three Feminist Perspectives on Anti-Semitism and Racism'*, New York, Long Haul Press, 1984, p. 18.

Bibliography

Archival sources for this study consisted of material held at the New South Wales State Archives, the Victorian Government Archives, the National Library of Australia, the Mitchell Library and the State Library of New South Wales, the La Trobe Library, the National Film and Sound Archives, the Performing Arts Museum of Victoria, University of Melbourne Archives, Sydney University Archives, the Powerhouse Museum, Coles-Myer Archives, the Australian Council of Educational Research Library and the Education Library, University of Melbourne. Also consulted were the Parliamentary Debates of Victoria and New South Wales, the Commonwealth Parliamentary Papers and the Reports of the Council of Public Education (Victoria).

Listed below are all primary sources, newspapers, magazines, pamphlets, films and contemporary publications specifically referred to in this book. In addition, I have listed those books, articles and unpublished material that I have drawn on in the argument of this book. I have not attempted to separate out this latter material from the publications of the 1950s and 1960s because the distinction is not always clear.

Books manuscripts and articles

Abel, E. *et al.* (eds) (1983) *The Voyage In: Fictions of Female Development.* Hanover, University Press of New England.

Abrams, M. (1959) *The Teenage Consumer.* London, The London Press Exchange Ltd.

Adams, P. and Minson, J. (1978) 'The "subject" of feminism', *M/F*, 2.

Allen, J. (1986) 'Evidence and silence: feminism and the limits of history', in C. Pateman and E. Gross (eds) *Feminist Challenges: Social and Political Theory.* Sydney, Allen and Unwin.

Ausubel, D.P. (1954) *Theory and Problems of Adolescent Development.* New York, Grune and Stratton.

Bakhtin, B. (1984) *Rabelais and his World.* Bloomington, Indiana University Press.

Bannister, H. (1986) 'Young male and delinquent: a juvenile delinquency panic in Victoria 1956'. Unpublished paper.

Barcan, A. (1972) 'The transition in Australian education 1939–67', in J. Cleverley and J. Lawry (eds) *Australian Education in the Twentieth Century*. Hawthorn, Longman.

Baruch, D.W. (1953) *How to Live with Your Teen-ager*. New York, McGraw-Hill.

de Beauvoir, S. (1972) *Brigitte Bardot and the Lolita Syndrome*. New York, Arno Press and *New York Times*.

Benhabib, S. (1987) 'The generalized and the concrete other: the Kohlberg–Gilligan controversy in feminist theory', in S. Benhabib and D. Cornell (eds), *Feminism as Critique: On the Politics of Gender*. Minneapolis, University of Minnesota Press.

Benhabib, S. and Cornell, D. (eds) (1987) Introduction to *Feminism as Critique*, Minneapolis, University of Minnesota Press.

Berman, M. (1985) *All that is Solid Melts into Air*. London, Verso.

Blackmore, J.A. (1986) 'Schooling for work: vocationalism in secondary education in Victoria.' PhD thesis, Stanford University.

Bolton, G. (1990) *The Middle Way: The Oxford History of Australia, Vol. 5, 1942–1988*. Melbourne, Oxford University Press.

Breines, W. (1986) 'The 1950s: gender and some social science', *Sociological Inquiry*, 56, 1.

Brown, M.E. (1990) 'Consumption and resistance – the problem of pleasure', in M.E. Brown (ed.) *Television and Women's Culture: The Politics of the Popular*. Sydney, Currency Press.

Burt, C. (1925) *The Young Delinquent*. London, University of London Press.

Campbell, W.J. (1962) *Television – and the Australian Adolescent*. Sydney, Angus and Robertson.

Clunies-Ross, I. (1956) 'The dilemma of modern education', *The Journal of Education*, 3, 3.

Cohen, P. (1986) 'Rethinking the youth question', *Working Paper 3*. Post-16 Education Centre, in association with Youth and Policy, London Institute of Education.

Cohen, S. (1972) *Folk Devils and Moral Panics: The Creation of the Mods and Rockers*. London, MacGibbon and Kee.

Cole, P. (ed.) (1935) *The Education of the Adolescent in Australia*. Melbourne, Australian Council of Educational Research.

Coleman, J.S. (1961) *The Adolescent Society: The Social Life of the Teenager and its Impact on Television*. New York, Free Press of Glencoe.

Connell, R.W. (1987) *Gender and Power*. Sydney, Allen and Unwin.

Connell, W.F. et al. (1959) *Growing Up in an Australian City: A Study of Adolescents in Sydney*. Melbourne, Australian Council of Educational Research.

Cunningham, K.S. (1951) 'Admissions requirements, tests and examinations', in P. Cole (ed.) *The Adjustment of Youth: A Study of a Social Problem in the British, American, and Australian Communities*. Melbourne, Melbourne University Press.

Curthoys, A. (1988) *For and Against Feminism. A Personal Journey into Feminist Theory and History*. Sydney, Allen and Unwin.

Doane, M.A. (1987) *The Desire to Desire: The Woman's Film of the 1940s.* Bloomington, Indiana University Press.

Docker, J. (1984) 'Culture, Society and the Communist Party', in A. Curthoys and J. Merritt (eds) *Australia's First Cold War, 1945–1953.* Sydney, Allen and Unwin.

Donzelot, J. (1979) *The Policing of Families*, R. Hurley (trans.), New York, Pantheon Books.

Dyhouse, C. (1981) *Girls Growing Up in Late Victorian and Edwardian England.* London, Routledge and Kegan Paul.

Ehrenreich, B. *et al.* (1986) 'Beatlemania: girls just want to have fun', in *Remaking Love: The Feminization of Sex.* London, Fontana.

Eisenstein, H. (1985) *Contemporary Feminist Thought.* Sydney, Allen and Unwin.

Ewen, S. (1976) *Captains of Consciousness: Advertising and the Social Roots of the Consumer Culture.* New York, McGraw-Hill.

Felski, R. (1989) *Beyond Feminist Aesthetics.* London, Hutchinson Radius.

Feminist History Group (1979) 'Feminism as femininity in the nineteen fifties?', *Feminist Review*, 3.

Finnane, M. (1989) 'Censorship and the child: explaining the comics campaign', *Australian Historical Studies*, 23, 92.

Fiske, J. (1989) 'Women and quiz shows: consumerism, patriarchy and resisting pleasures', in M.E. Brown (ed.) *Television and Women's Culture: The Politics of the Popular.* Sydney, Currency Press.

Foucault, M. (1977) In D.F. Bouchard (ed.) *Language, Counter-Memory, Practice: Selected Essays and Interviews*, D.F. Bouchard and S. Simon (trans). Oxford, Basil Blackwell.

Foucault, M. (1988) 'Technologies of the self', in L.H. Martin (ed.) *Technologies of the Self: A Seminar with Michel Foucault.* London, Tavistock Publications.

Foucault, M. (1988) In L.D. Kritzman (ed.) *Politics, Philosophy, Culture: Interviews and Other Writings, 1977–1984.* New York, Routledge.

Fraser, N. (1985) 'What's critical about critical theory? The case of Habermas and gender', *New German Critique*, 35.

French, E.L. (ed.) (1964) *Melbourne Studies in Education.* Melbourne, Melbourne University Press.

Friedan, B. (1983) *The Feminine Mystique.* Harmondsworth, Penguin.

Friedenburg, E.Z. (1959) *The Vanishing Adolescent.* Boston, Beacon Press.

Frisby, D. (1985) *Fragments of Modernity: Theories of Modernity in the Work of Simmel, Kracauer and Benjamin.* Cambridge, Polity Press.

Gerster, R. and Bassett, J. (1991) *Seizures of Youth: The Sixties and Australia.* Melbourne, Hyland House.

Gill, P.N. (1964) 'The Federal Science Grant: an episode in church and state relations, 1963–1964', in E.L. French (ed.) *Melbourne Studies in Education.* Melbourne, Melbourne University Press.

Gilligan, C. (1982) *In a Different Voice.* Cambridge, Mass., Harvard University Press.

Gilligan, C. (1986) 'Remapping the moral domain: new images of the self in relationship', in T. Heller *et al.* (eds) *Reconstructing Individu-*

alism: Autonomy, Individuality, and the Self in Western Thought.
Stanford, Calif., Stanford University Press.

Goodman, P. (1961) *Growing Up Absurd: Problems of Youth in the Organ-ized System.* London, Victor Gollancz.

Greer, G. (1989) 'Greer at 50: on growing old but not growing up', *Vogue,* January, London.

Grosz, E. (1990) *Jacques Lacan: A Feminist Introduction.* Sydney, Allen and Unwin.

Grumley, J. (1992) 'Two views of the paradigm of production', *Praxis International,* 12, 2.

Gurley Brown, H. (1963) *Sex and the Single Girl.* London, Frederick Muller.

Habermas, J. (1985) 'Modernity – An incomplete project', in H. Foster (ed.) *Postmodern Culture.* London, Pluto Press.

Hall, S. (1990) 'The emergence of cultural studies and the crisis of the humanities', *October,* 53.

Hall, S. and Jefferson, T. (eds) (1976) *Resistance through Rituals.* London, Hutchinson.

Harvey, D. (1989) *The Condition of Postmodernity: An Enquiry into the Origins of Cultural Change.* London, Basil Blackwell.

Havighurst, R.J. (1953) *Human Development and Education.* New York, Longmans, Green and Co.

Heller, A. (1982/3) 'The dissatisfied society', *Praxis International,* 2.

Henriques, J. *et al.* (eds) (1984) *Changing the Subject.* London, Methuen.

Hoggart, R. (1957) *The Uses of Literacy.* London, Chatto and Windus.

Horne, D. (1964) *The Lucky Country.* Harmondsworth, Penguin.

Horne, D. (1987) *The Lucky Country Revisited.* Melbourne, Dent.

Hunter, I. (1988) *Culture and Government: The Emergence of Literary Education.* London, Macmillan.

Huyssen, A. (1986) 'Mass culture as woman: modernism's other', in T. Modleski (ed.) *Studies in Entertainment: Critical Approaches to Mass Culture.* Bloomington, Indiana University Press.

Huyssen, A. (1990) 'Mapping the postmodern', in L. Nicholson (ed.) *Feminism and Postmodernism.* New York, Routledge.

Hyams, B.K. and Bessant, B. (1972) *Schools for the People?* Hawthorn, Longman.

Jameson, F. (1985) 'Postmodernism and consumer society', in H. Foster (ed.) *Postmodern Culture.* London, Pluto Press.

Jephcott, A.P. (1942) *Girls Growing Up.* London, Faber and Faber.

Johnson, L. (1990) 'Gender issues and education', *Australian Feminist Studies,* 11.

Johnson, P. (1992) 'Quest for the self: feminism's appropriation of romanticism.' Unpublished paper delivered at the Department of General Philosophy Seminar, University of Sydney.

Johnston, G. (1964) *My Brother Jack: A Novel.* London, Collins.

Ker Conway, J. (1989) *The Road to Coorain: An Australian Memoir.* London, Heinemann.

Larrain, J. (1979) *The Concept of Ideology.* London, Hutchinson.

de Lauretis, T. (1989) *Technologies of Gender: Essays on Theory, Film and Fiction.* Bloomington, Indiana University Press.

178   *The modern girl*

Lees, S. and Senyard, J. (1987) *The 1950s . . . How Australia Became a Modern Society, and Everyone got a House and a Car*. Melbourne, Hyland House.
Lefebvre, H. (1971) *Everyday Life in the Modern World*. Sacha Rabinovitch (trans.), New York, Harper Torchbooks.
Mackenzie, N. (1962) *Women in Australia*. Melbourne, F.W. Cheshire.
Manning, A.E. (1958) *The Bodgie: A Study in Psychological Abnormality*, Sydney, Angus and Robertson.
Markus, M. (1987) 'Women, success and civil society: submission to, or subversion of, the Achievement Principle', in S. Benhabib and D. Cornell (eds), *Feminism as Critique: On the Politics of Gender*. Minneapolis, University of Minnesota Press.
Martin, B. and Mohanty, C.T. (1988) 'Feminist politics: what's home got to do with it?', in T. de Lauretis (ed.) *Feminist Studies/Critical Studies*. London, Macmillan.
Matthews, J. (1986) 'Feminist history', *Labour History*, 50.
Maunders, D. (1984) *Keeping them off the Streets*. Melbourne, Phillip Institute of Technology.
Minson, J. (1985) *Genealogies of Morals: Nietzsche, Foucault, Donzelot and the Eccentricity of Ethics*. London, Macmillan.
Mohanty, C. (1988) 'Under western eyes: feminist scholarship and colonial discourses', *Feminist Review*, 30.
Moretti, F. (1987) *The Way of the World: The* Bildungsroman *in European Culture*. London, Verso.
Morris, M. (1988a) 'Banality in cultural studies', *Discourse*, X.2.
Morris, M. (1988b) 'Things to do with shopping centres', in S. Sheridan (ed.) *Grafts: Feminist Cultural Criticism*. London, Verso.
Mulvey, L. (1991) 'A phantasmagoria of the female body: the work of Cindy Sherman', *New Left Review*, 188.
Nava, M. (1987) 'Consumerism and its contradictions', *Cultural Studies*, 1, 2.
Nava, M. (1991) 'Consumerism reconsidered: buying and power', *Cultural Studies*, 5, 2.
Newsom, J. (1948) *The Education of Girls*. London, Faber and Faber.
Oakley, A. (1984) *Taking it Like a Woman*. London, Fontana.
Oeser, O.A. (ed.) (1955) *Teacher, Pupil and Task: Elements of Social Psychology Applied to Education*. London, Tavistock Publications.
Oeser, O.A. and Hammond, S.B. (eds) (1954) *Social Structure and Personality in a City*. London, Routledge and Kegan Paul.
Owens, C. (1985) 'The discourse of others: feminists and postmodernism', in H. Foster (ed.) *Postmodern Culture*. London, Pluto Press.
Palmer, I. (ed.) (1984) *Melbourne Studies in Education*. Melbourne, Melbourne University Press.
Pateman, C. (1981) 'The concept of equity', in P.N. Troy (ed.) *A Just Society? Essays on Equity in Australia*. Sydney, Allen and Unwin.
Pearson, J. and Turner, G. (1965) *The Persuasion Industry*. London, Eyre and Spottiswoode.
Petro, P. (1987) 'Modernity and mass culture in Weimar: contours of a discourse on sexuality in early theories of perception and representation', *New German Critique*, 40.

Petro, P. (1989) *Joyless Streets: Women and Melodramatic Representation in Weimar Germany*. Princeton, Princeton University Press.

Phillips, A.A. (1958) *The Australian Tradition: Studies in a Colonial Culture*. Melbourne, Cheshire.

Phillips, A.A. (1962) 'The schools', in P. Coleman (ed.) *Australian Civilization*. Melbourne, F.W. Cheshire.

Pratt, M.N. (1984) 'Identity: skin blood heart', in E. Bulkin *et al.* (eds) *Yours in Struggle: Three Feminist Perspectives on Anti-Semitism and Racism*. New York, Long Haul Press.

Pumphrey, M. (1987) 'The flapper, the housewife and the making of modernity', *Cultural Studies*, 1, 2.

Radway, J. (1984) *Reading the Romance: Women, Patriarchy, and Popular Literature*. Chapel Hill, University of North Carolina Press.

Riesman, D. (1950) *The Lonely Crowd: A Study of the Changing American Character*. New Haven, Conn., Yale University Press.

Riley, D. (1983) *War in the Nursery: Theories of the Child and Mother*. London, Virago.

Riley, D. (1988) *'Am I that Name?' Feminism and the Category of 'Women' in History*. Minneapolis, University of Minnesota Press.

Rose, N. (1990) 'Psychology as a "Social" Science', in I. Parker and J. Shotter (eds) *Deconstructing Social Psychology*. London, Routledge.

Rowbotham, S. (1973) *Woman's Consciousness, Man's World*. Harmondsworth, Penguin.

Rowbotham, S. (1989) *The Past is Before Us: Feminism in Action since the 1960s*. London, Pandora.

Russo, M. (1988) 'Female grotesques: carnival and theory', in T. de Lauretis (ed.) *Feminist Studies/Critical Studies*. London, Macmillan.

Scott, J.W. (1988) *Gender and the Politics of History*. New York, Columbia University Press.

Smart, D. (1984) 'The Industrial Fund: A highly successful model of big business collaboration with the Headmasters' Conference in the interests of school science', in I. Palmer (ed.) *Melbourne Studies in Education*. Melbourne, Melbourne University Press.

Spearritt, P. (1978) *Sydney Since the Twenties*. Sydney, Hale and Iremonger.

Steedman, C. (1982) *The Tidy House: Little Girls Writing*. London, Virago.

Teese, R. (1984) 'The evolution of the Victorian secondary school system', in L. Johnson and D. Tyler (eds) *Cultural Politics: Papers in Contemporary Australian Education, Culture and Politics*, Melbourne Working Papers, Vol. 5.

Thom D. (1987) 'Better a teacher than a hairdresser? "A mad passion for equality" or keeping Molly and Betty down', in F. Hunt (ed.) *Lessons for Life: The Schooling of Girls and Women, 1850–1950*. Oxford, Basil Blackwell.

Toulmin, S. (1990) *Cosmopolis: The Hidden Agenda of Modernity*. New York, Free Press.

Townsend, H. (1988) *The Baby Boomers: Growing up in Australia in the 1940s, 50s and 60s*. Brookvale, Simon Schuster.

Victorian Secondary Teachers' Association (1965) *The Secondary Teacher*, 102, February.

Walkerdine, V. (1984) 'Developmental psychology and the child-centred pedagogy: the insertion of Piaget into early education', in J. Henriques *et al.* (eds) *Changing the Subject: Psychology, Social Regulation and Subjectivity.* London, Methuen.

Ward, R. (1958) *The Australian Legend.* Melbourne, Oxford University Press.

Weeks, J. (1991) 'Invented Moralities', *History Workshop*, 32.

Whitwell, G. (1989) *Making the Market: The Rise of the Consumer Society.* Melbourne, McPhee Gribble.

Williamson, J. (1983) 'Images of "woman" – The photographs of Cindy Sherman', *Screen*, 24, 6.

Williamson, J. (1986) 'The problems of being popular', *New Socialist*, 41, September.

Winship, J. (1982) 'Woman becomes an "individual" – femininity and consumption in women's magazines, 1954–69.' Centre for Contemporary Cultural Studies, Stencilled Occasional Paper.

Wolpe, A.M. (1974) 'The official ideology of education for girls', in M. Flude and J. Ahier (eds) *Educability, Schools and Ideology.* New York, John Wiley.

Young, I.M. (1989) 'Throwing like a girl: a phenomenology of feminine body comportment, motility and spatiality', in J. Allen and I.M. Young (eds) *The Thinking Muse: Feminism and Modern French Philosophy.* Bloomington, Indiana University Press.

Zainuddin, A.G.T. (1982) *They Dreamt of a School: A Centenary History of Methodist Ladies College Kew 1882–1982.* Melbourne, Hyland House.

Films

Cinesound Review, Issue No. 1131, 3 July 1953, National Sound Archives, Canberra.

Field, Connie (1980) 'The Life and Times of Rosie the Riveter', Franklin Lakes, N.J., Clarity Educational Productions.

Jaffe, Rona (1959) 'The Best of Everything'. Twentieth Century Fox.

McMurchy, Megan *et al.* (*c.*1983) 'For Love or Money': A history of women and work in Australia, Flashback Films.

Commissions of inquiry, parliamentary papers and archival sources cited

Australian Council of Educational Research (1956) *The Shire of Ferntree Gully and its Educational Future.* Melbourne, ACER.

Report of Juvenile Delinquency Advisory Committee (Justice Barry, Chair). Report to Hon. Rylah, MLA, Chief Secretary of Victoria, 17 July 1956 (Barry Report).

Connell, W.F. (1973) 'Trends in Educational Research Since World War Two', Presidential Address to the Australian Association for Educational Research, W.F. Connell Papers, University of Sydney Archives.

Girls, Schools and Society (1975) Report published by the Commonwealth Schools Commission, Canberra.

Report of the Consultative Committee on the Education of the Adolescent. Board of Education, London, HMSO, 1926 (Hadow Report).

Hood, D.W. (1952) 'A Critical Evaluation of Youth Education in Australia', typewritten manuscript held at the University of Melbourne, Education Library.

'Interim Report of Council to Minister of Public Instruction: Educational Reform', The Council of Public Education (Victoria), 33rd Annual Report, 1943.

Report of the Committee Appointed to Survey Secondary Education in New South Wales (Wyndham Report), 1957.

Report of the Committee on State Education in Victoria (Ramsay Report), 1960.

Submissions and Exhibits to *Survey of Secondary Education* (1955), New South Wales State Archives.

Australia, House of Representatives (1962) *Debates*, Vols 34, 36, 37.

Newspapers and magazines

Age
Australian Women's Weekly
Broadcasting and Television
Listener In
Listener In – TV
Myer News
New Idea
Rydge's
Sun-Herald
Sydney Morning Herald
Teen Twenty
Teenage
Teenage and Women's Wear
Teenage Topics
The Secondary Teacher

Pamphlets cited

A Guide to Womanhood, Sydney, Father and Son Welfare Movement, 1960/62.

'Cosmetics – The fragrant jungle', *Current Affairs Bulletin* 25, 5, University of Sydney, 1960.

E. Millis Duval, *The Art of Dating*, n.d.

On Becoming a Woman, Warburton, Victoria, Signs Publishing Company, n.d.

The Guide to 'Teen Years', Sydney, Father and Son Welfare Movement, 1959.

Index